I0803749

IMAGES
of America

ATLANTIC BEACH

On the Cover: These three men with their backs to the viewer are in the timeless pursuit of fishing that is typical of many other idyllic spots around the world. They are unique, however, because they toil during the Depression era at a segregated oceanfront for blacks only—Atlantic Beach. The full version of this image (see page 25) includes four men. (Lenwood Lewis.)

IMAGES
of America

ATLANTIC BEACH

Sherry A. Suttles
The Atlantic Beach Historical Society

ARCADIA
PUBLISHING

ISBN 978-0-7385-6820-1

Published by Arcadia Publishing
Charleston, South Carolina

Printed in the United States of America

Library of Congress Control Number: 2008942611

For all general information contact Arcadia Publishing at:
Telephone 843-853-2070
Fax 843-853-0044
E-mail sales@arcadiapublishing.com
For customer service and orders:
Toll-Free 1-888-313-2665

Visit us on the Internet at www.arcadiapublishing.com

To my late mother and father, Ann E. and Nathaniel Suttles, who taught me the love of black history and tried to teach me fishing

Contents

Acknowledgments		6
Introduction		7
1.	Segregation: Founders, Community, and Pillars	9
2.	Heyday: Buses, Bikers, Dining, and Dancing to R&B Music	43
3.	Integration: The Town and Revitalization Efforts	95
About the Organization		126
Index		127
Bibliography		127

Acknowledgments

First, I thank God for bringing me to Atlantic Beach and helping me to preserve its history. Further, I thank my son Kamau Suttles and other family members from afar.

Next, I thank the founders of the Atlantic Beach Historical Society (ABHS)—"outsiders" who cared: Carolyn Marie Sadler and her husband, Thomas "Pop" Sadler from Charlotte; James Goodman and James Williams from Florence; and Johanna Martin-Carrington (Jenkins Institute) and James French (*Chronicle*) from Charleston. I thank early supporter Betty "Toby" Dixon, cochair of the Atlantic Beach Chamber of Commerce with Brian Shaw. I salute second ABHS president Latonia Peterson, who stepped in when I ran for town council.

Also thanks go to early funders Drew Hansen, Conway National Bank; Mary Ann Corbett, Wachovia Bank; Larry Brumfield, LWB Development Group; Waccamaw Foundation; South Carolina Humanities Council; City of Myrtle Beach; Lee Renfro, Wal-Mart, North Myrtle Beach; William "Pete" Johnson Jr. and Melvin Ware, NMB Drag Strip; Nick Patel, Budget Inn; Joe Chestnut; Bill Parrott, Crazy Horse; and Beth Hughes, Pepsi; E&E Motel; Paul Curry; Brian Shaw; Drs. H. H., Ed, and Noble Cooper; Kelly Group; Marathon Development; and LaCasa.

Thanks to board members Rosa Stanley, cochair; Brenda Rowell-Bromell, cochair; Tema Lewis Hill, secretary; Dorothy Carmichael Floyd, treasurer; and Retha Pierce, parliamentarian.

I thank participants in the Oral History Project—Professors Damon Fordham, College of Charleston, Avery, and Veronica Davis Gerald, Coastal Carolina University; the elders: Etrulia Dozier, Alice Graham, Jannie and Willie Isom, Abraham Jenkins, William "Pete" Johnson Sr. and Jr., Katie Powell, Carrine Rucker, Russell Skeeters, Emma Lee Vereen, and Earlene Woods; and Avery Research Center, Charleston, the ABHS archival collection.

Thanks to all residents, including Josephine Isom, Horry County Register of Deeds. My most sincere gratitude is extended to all the families who entrusted me with their fragile vintage photographs, to Johnson C. Smith University, and Fayetteville State University. And much thanks to the North Myrtle Beach Library.

I extend my greatest thanks posthumously to the late Tim Martin, who architected the Grandfather Plan and whose Web site www.abhistory.org links to Atlantic Beach photographs on www.Flickr.com; and to the Beach Lady, who showed me the value of keeping prime oceanfront undeveloped, if need be, to keep a majority of it for African American posterity.

Much appreciation to Arcadia Publishing's Lindsay Harris, Maggie Bullwinkel, and David Mandel.

Sherry A. Suttles is solely responsible for this work for any omissions or commissions. Requests to make changes or be excluded were honored, and permission slips are on file.

Photograph Credits, in Order of First Appearance: Lenwood (son of Jim) Lewis; Hazel Ballen Eagles (niece of Roxie Ballen Tyson); Barbara Ballen (niece of Roxie Ballen Tyson); Johnson C. Smith University/Fayetteville State University (Seabrook photograph and Gertha Gibson dissertation); Doris Covington (friend of Dr. Robert K. Gordon); Michael Kelly (son of Dr. Peter C. Kelly III); Horry County Deeds; South Carolina Secretary of State; H. H. Cooper Jr. (nephew of Dr. Robert K. Gordon); Fay Porter (widow of Yaro Stropnicky); William Pete Johnson Jr. (son); Willa DeWitt; Dorothy C. Floyd (daughter of Jerry Carmichael); Rosa Stanley; Curt Teich Archives; Brenda Rowell-Bromell (Hotel Marshall); Avery Research Center; Atlantic Beach Historical Society/Avery; Mildred Daniels McKoy (daughter); Billy Scott; Tema Lewis Hill; Barbara Fordham Collier (granddaughter); Delois Gore Jenerette (daughter); Halestine Tyson Cox; Russell Skeeters (son); Earlene Woods; *Charleston Chronicle*; Robert Simpson (E&E owner); Amy Breunig (motel owner); Samuella Williams Holmes; Horry County Museum

INTRODUCTION

ATLANTIC BEACH
SOUTH CAROLINA HISTORICAL MARKER 162

Atlantic Beach, nicknamed "The Black Pearl," was established about 1934 as an oceanfront community for blacks denied access to other area beaches by segregation. Many became year-round residents, but most spent their vacations here. From the 1930s to the 1970s "The Black Pearl" was one of the most popular beach resorts on the East Coast for blacks from Va. to Fla. Its hotels, nightclubs, restaurants, shops, and pavilion were packed every May to September.

George Tyson was the first to develop this area, from 1934 to 1943. In 1943 the Atlantic Beach Co.—J. W. Seabrook, R. K. Gordon, and P. C. Kelly III—bought the tracts and continued to develop them. As other area beaches began desegregating in the 1970s the beach saw fewer visitors. The town of Atlantic Beach, chartered in 1966 with Emery Gore and Millard Rucker as its first two mayors, is one of a few black-owned and governed oceanfront communities in the United States.

—Approved April 12, 2005, by J. Tracy Power, Ph.D., coordinator, South Carolina Historical Marker Program, South Carolina Department of Archives and History, this marker was erected by the Atlantic Beach Historical Society, May 22, 2005, at the town hall, at Thirtieth and Atlantic Avenues in Atlantic Beach.

There have been six mayors from 1966 to the present: Emery Gore, Millard Rucker, Joe Montgomery, Cleveland Stevens, Irene Armstrong, and Retha Pierce. There have been over a dozen town managers since 1996, most serving only six months: Pete Johnson Jr., Mervyl McMillan (four years), Diane Poston, Al Harvey, Linda Angus, Carolyn Montgomery (four years), Marcia Conner, and Charles Williams (twice). The town has never applied for, nor received recognition as, a council-manager form of government by the International City-County Management Association. Except for a two-year absence, Cheryl Pereira has served as clerk since Pete Johnson hired her in 1996. Jacqui Gore Woods is also on the staff. Mayor Retha Pierce won a long court battle to preside over the current council—Charlene Taylor, mayor pro tem; Donnell Thompson; and Jake Evans.

After September 11, 2001, Atlantic Beach streets became numbered. Tyson, Atlantic, Carolina, and Virginia became Twenty-ninth, Thirtieth, Thirty-first, and Thirty-second Avenues, respectively. A redevelopment map of 2001 shows residential uses for Twenty-ninth and Thirty-second, commercial uses for Thirtieth, Thirty-first, and Highway 17; ocean (waterfront) resort uses. All cities cited are in South Carolina, unless specified differently.

Atlantic Beach
Five Years from Today

I visited Atlantic Beach in my dreams last night—
and what I found there had to come from a struggle, a fight.
As I turned down main street it was a sight to see—
what I saw meant so much to its people and me.
There were cars everywhere, no spaces to park—
as I drove thru, the finished product just filled my heart.
Businesses open, people everywhere—
the pride within them, heavy in the air.
Truck filling orders before the shops ran out—
success was everywhere as visitors moved about.
There were marquees telling of entertainment to come—
everybody was busy welcoming all kinds of someone's.
Oh! the beach was still owned mostly by black women and men—
but they were sharing this with other minorities that had also bought in.
The beach property was filled with all kinds of people having good fun—
Atlantic Beach had arrived now it was #1.
I stopped at the little CME church that had been newly built on the right—
and the memories took me back to the beginning of the struggle, the fight.
A lot of things had changed in this little black town—
the strength within it made a loud sound.
As I sat there I could see who had the majority—
and it felt good the way things turned out to be.
It had been 5 yrs. with nothing but struggle along the way—
and as I sat there, I thanked God,
for letting the people of this little town, make it to today . . .

—by Patricia Robinson
October 29, 2005

American Beach, on Amelia Island, Florida, salutes our "sister city," Atlantic Beach, South Carolina, on the celebration of their 75th diamond anniversary of its establishment in 1934. So many thanks to Sherry Suttles and the Atlantic Beach Historical Society for this masterful document.

—Marsha Dean Phelts
author of *An American Beach for African Americans*
and *The American Beach Cookbook*

One

Segregation

Founders, Community, and Pillars

Roxie Ballen Tyson (1889–1973) was wife and business partner to George W. Tyson. She was a very successful seamstress. George W. Tyson (1890–1967), a naval reservist in World War I from Wilmington, North Carolina, was an entrepreneur who operated a Conway cleaners and laundromat. He bought the Atlantic Beach land with family money, according to nieces Barbara Ballen and Hazel Ballen Eagles. (Hazel Ballen Eagles.)

Carlton Ballen, Roxie's brother, was photographed by renowned James Van Der Zee. There are no available pictures of his brother-in-law Tyson, who is remembered as having chestnut-brown skin, of average height, and with high intelligence, drive, and ambition. H. H. Singleton, of the Conway NAACP, remembers Tyson as "an outspoken visionary and champion for his people and the cause, which was Atlantic Beach." (Barbara Ballen.)

Mattie Ballen, Carlton's wife and Roxie's sister-in-law, now age 90, used to visit Atlantic Beach often when health permitted, says her daughter Barbara. The Ballen family helped fund the "exploits" of their dapper, do-gooder in-law, George W. Tyson. (Ballen.)

James Ward Seabrook, Ph.D., (1886–1974) was among the first 10 buyers of lots at $300 in 1936 from G. W. Tyson. Later he became president of the Atlantic Beach Company. (Johnson C. Smith University and Fayetteville State University.)

Dr. Robert Keith Gordon (1893–1964), treasurer and vice president of Atlantic Beach Company, obtained his medical degree from Howard University. He went to Mayo High School in Darlington and Claflin College in Orangeburg. His wife, Mayme Sawyer Gordon, and her eight siblings also attended Claflin. Mayme and her father, Edward James Sawyer, were on the board of trustees of Claflin and also the United Methodist Church USA. Mayme and her three sisters from Bennettsville (Gertrude, Mildred, and Ada) all married doctors. Dr. Gordon was the first African American physician in Dillon County. (Doris Covington.)

Dr. Peter Carlisle Kelly III (1911–1980) bought land from Tyson and became secretary of the Atlantic Beach Company. Born in Georgetown, Dr. Kelly is a Howard University graduate. He had many civic accomplishments, such as serving as president of the NAACP, but he was "best known as the only black physician who served people of all races tirelessly," wrote Etrulia Dozier in the *Independent Quarterly*. (Michael Kelly.)

Peter Carlisle Kelly II was Dr. Kelly's father. "Wealthy men from England, mostly, colonized Horry County. They had huge parcels given to them by the Kings and Queens and came to realize: 'One cannot eat land. It has to be made to produce or be sold'," writes Dr. A. Goff Bedford in the *Independent Republic*. The Bells owned most of Crescent Beach, reports Catherine Lewis in *Horry County, South Carolina, 1730–2003*. (Kelly.)

Juanita Thelma Lynch Kelly (1922–2003), a native of Conway, graduated from Whittemore High School and South Carolina State College. She helped her husband, Dr. Kelly III, at their Kelly Clinic and was a member of Cherry Hill Baptist Church. The Kellys have five children: daughter Demetra and sons Patrick, Michael, Peter IV, and Anthony. (Kelly.)

Catherine Kelly, Dr. Kelly III's mother, purchased Tyson land in her name as C. T. Kelly. The Kelly Group owns the most Atlantic Beach parcels (23). According to Blanche Floyd's *Tales along the King's Highway*, Atlantic Beach names seem derived from "the independent-minded 1700 settlers, though blacks were freed early from slavery as cotton, then timber became the mainstay": Gordon (Scottish); Evans, Owens, Lewis, and Thomas (Welsh); Vaught (German); and Vereen and Bellamy (French Huguenots). (Kelly.)

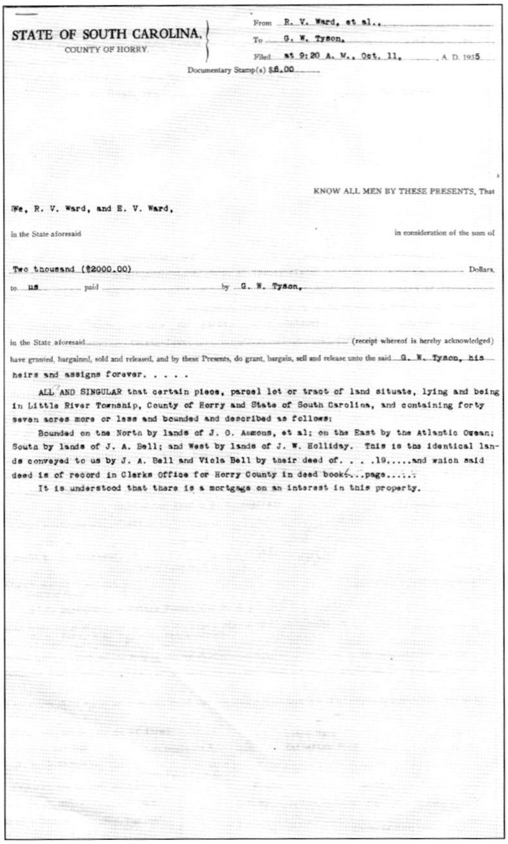

STATE OF SOUTH CAROLINA,
COUNTY OF HORRY

From R. V. Ward, et al.,
To G. W. Tyson,
Filed at 9:20 A. M., Oct. 11, A. D. 1935
Documentary Stamp(s) $6.00

KNOW ALL MEN BY THESE PRESENTS, That We, R. V. Ward, and E. V. Ward, in the State aforesaid in consideration of the sum of Two thousand ($2000.00) Dollars, to us paid by G. W. Tyson, in the State aforesaid (receipt whereof is hereby acknowledged) have granted, bargained, sold and released, and by these Presents, do grant, bargain, sell and release unto the said G. W. Tyson, his heirs and assigns forever. . . . .

ALL AND SINGULAR that certain piece, parcel lot or tract of land situate, lying and being in Little River Township, County of Horry and State of South Carolina, and containing forty seven acres more or less and bounded and described as follows:

Bounded on the North by lands of J. O. Ammons, et al; on the East by the Atlantic Ocean; South by lands of J. A. Bell; and West by lands of J. W. Holliday. This is the identical lands conveyed to us by J. A. Bell and Viola Bell by their deed of. . . .19.....and which said deed is of record in Clerks Office for Horry County in deed book...page.....

It is understood that there is a mortgage on an interest in this property.

R. V. Ward sold land to George W. Tyson on October 11, 1934, for $2,000, according to this deed. The Bell family, which owned much of Crescent Beach (as detailed in *Horry County, South Carolina: 1730–1993* by Catherine H. Lewis), had sold the parcel to Ward. Neither expected Tyson to honor the mortgage, and they were quite surprised, said Ila Pearl Bell Bosley, that he did so. This first "Atlantic Beach" tract, now Twenty-ninth and Thirtieth Avenues, was 47 acres. (Horry County Deeds.)

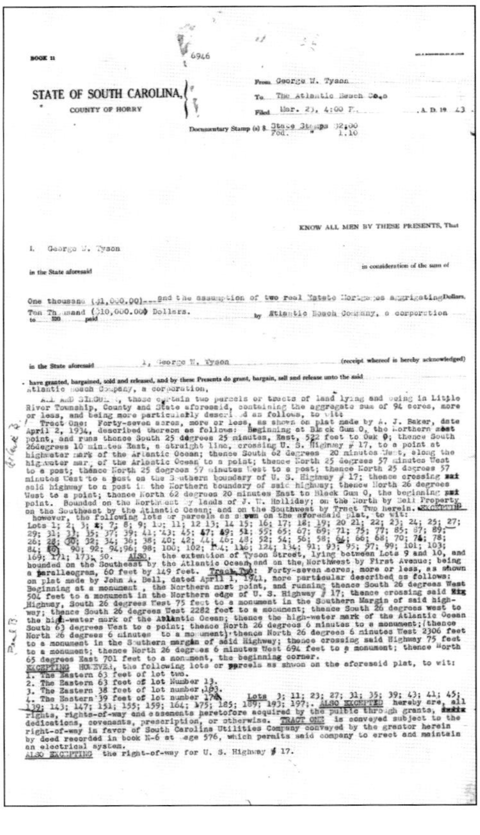

BOOK 11 6946

STATE OF SOUTH CAROLINA,
COUNTY OF HORRY

From George W. Tyson
To The Atlantic Beach Co.,
Filed Mar. 29, 4:00 P. A. D. 19 43
Documentary Stamp (s) $ State Stamps $2.00 Fed. " 1.10

KNOW ALL MEN BY THESE PRESENTS, That I, George W. Tyson in the State aforesaid in consideration of the sum of One thousand ($1,000.00)---and the assumption of two real Estate Mortgages aggregating Ten Thousand ($10,000.00) Dollars, to me paid by Atlantic Beach Company, a corporation in the State aforesaid I, George W. Tyson (receipt whereof is hereby acknowledged) have granted, bargained, sold and released, and by these Presents do grant, bargain, sell and release unto the said Atlantic Beach Company, a corporation,

ALL AND SINGULAR, those certain two parcels or tracts of land lying and being in Little River Township, County and State aforesaid, containing the aggregate sum of 94 acres, more or less, and being more particularly described as follows, to wit:

Tract One: Forty-seven acres, more or less, as shown on plat made by A. J. Baker, date April 2, 1934, described thereon as follows: Beginning at Black Gum O, the Northern most point, and runs thence South 25 degrees 25 minutes, East, 522 feet to Oak O; thence South 26degrees 10 minutes East, a straight line, crossing U. S. Highway # 17, to a point at highwater mark of the Atlantic Ocean; thence South 62 degrees 20 minutes West, along the highwater mark of the Atlantic Ocean to a point; thence North 25 degrees 57 minutes West to a post; thence North 25 degrees 57 minutes West to a post; thence North 25 degrees 57 minutes West to a post on the Southern boundary of U. S. Highway # 17; thence crossing said highway to a post in the Northern boundary of said highway; thence North 26 degrees West to a point; thence North 62 degrees 20 minutes East to Black Gum O, the beginning point. Bounded on the Northwest by lands of J. W. Holliday; on the North by Bell Property on the Southeast by the Atlantic Ocean; and on the Southwest by Tract Two herein. EXCEPTING however, the following lots or parcels as shown on the aforesaid plat, to wit: Lots 1; 2; 3; 4; 7; 8; 9; 10; 11; 12 13; 14 15; 16; 17; 18; 19; 20 21; 22; 23; 24; 25; 27; 29; 31; 33; 35; 37; 39; 41; 43; 45; 47; 49; 51; 55; 65; 67; 69; 71; 75; 77; 85; 87; 89; 26; 28; 30; 32; 34; 36; 38; 40; 42; 44; 46; 48; 52; 54; 56; 58; 64; 66; 68; 70; 74; 78; 84; 80; 90; 92; 94;96; 98; 100; 102; 104; 116; 124; 134; 91; 93; 95; 97; 99; 101; 103; 169; 171; 173; 50. ALSO, the extention of Tyson Street, lying between Lots 9 and 10, and bounded on the Southeast by the Atlantic Ocean and on the Northwest by First Avenue; being a parallelogram, 60 feet by 149 feet. Tract Two: Forty-seven acres, more or less, as shown on plat made by John A. Bell, dated April 1, 1941, more particular described as follows: Beginning at a monument , the Northern most point, and running thence South 26 degrees West 504 feet to a monument in the Northern edge of U. S. Highway # 17; thence crossing said Highway, South 26 degrees West 75 feet to a monument in the Southern Margin of said highway; thence South 26 degrees West 2282 feet to a monument; thence South 26 degrees west to the high-water mark of the Atlantic Ocean; thence the high-water mark of the Atlantic Ocean South 63 degrees West to a point; thence North 26 degrees 6 minutes to a monument; (thence North 26 degrees 6 minutes to a monument) thence North 26 degrees 6 minutes West 2306 feet to a monument in the Southern margin of said Highway; thence crossing said Highway 75 feet to a monument; thence North 26 degrees 6 minutes West 694 feet to a monument; thence North 65 degrees East 701 feet to a monument, the beginning corner.

EXCEPTING HOWEVER, the following lots or parcels as shwon on the aforesaid plat, to wit:
1. The Eastern 63 feet of lot two.
2. The Eastern 63 feet of lot Number 13.
3. The Eastern 38 feet of lot number 183.
4. The Eastern 39 feet of lot number 174. Lots 3; 11; 23; 27; 31; 35; 39; 43; 41; 45; 139; 143; 147; 151; 155; 159; 164; 175; 185; 189; 193; 197;. ALSO EXCEPTED hereby are, all rights, rights-of-way and easements heretofore acquired by the public through grants, dedications, covenants, prescription, or otherwise. TRACT ONE is conveyed subject to the right-of-way in favor of South Carolina Utilities Company conveyed by the grantor herein by deed recorded in book N-6 at page 576, which permits said company to erect and maintain an electrical system.

ALSO EXCEPTING the right-of-way for U. S. Highway # 17.

In 1943, Tyson deeded over property, for $1,000 and assumption of two real estate mortgages aggregating $10,000, that he was developing for nine years to the Atlantic Beach Company—doctors who had purchased his 50-by-150-foot lots. Some say he ran into financial difficulties, but it was a myth that a white farmer named Spivey gave him the land to develop for black maids. (Horry County Deeds.)

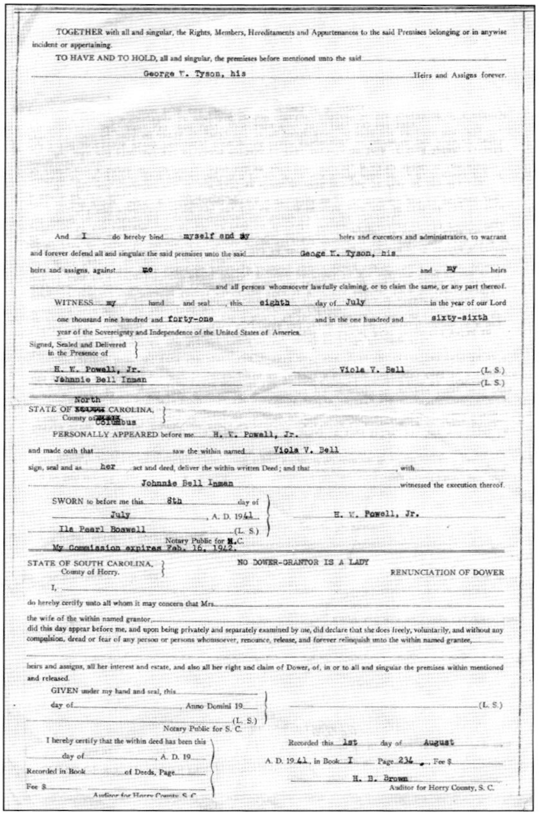

TOGETHER with all and singular, the Rights, Members, Hereditaments and Appurtenances to the said Premises belonging or in anywise incident or appertaining.

TO HAVE AND TO HOLD, all and singular, the premises before mentioned unto the said George V. Tyson, his Heirs and Assigns forever.

And I do hereby bind myself and my heirs and executors and administrators, to warrant and forever defend all and singular the said premises unto the said Geoge V. Tyson, his heirs and assigns, against me and my heirs and all persons whomsoever lawfully claiming, or to claim the same, or any part thereof.

WITNESS my hand and seal, this eighth day of July in the year of our Lord one thousand nine hundred and forty-one and in the one hundred and sixty-sixth year of the Sovereignty and Independence of the United States of America.

Signed, Sealed and Delivered in the Presence of

H. V. Powell, Jr.
Johnnie Bell Inman

Viola V. Bell (L. S.)
(L. S.)

STATE OF North CAROLINA,
County of Columbus

PERSONALLY APPEARED before me H. V. Powell, Jr. and made oath that saw the within named Viola V. Bell sign, seal and as her act and deed, deliver the within written Deed; and that , with Johnnie Bell Inman witnessed the execution thereof.

SWORN to before me this 8th day of July, A. D. 1941

Ila Pearl Boswell (L. S.)
Notary Public for N.C.
My Commission expires Feb. 16, 1942.

H. V. Powell, Jr.

STATE OF SOUTH CAROLINA,
County of Horry.

NO DOWER-GRANTOR IS A LADY

RENUNCIATION OF DOWER

I,

do hereby certify unto all whom it may concern that Mrs.

the wife of the within named grantor,

did this day appear before me, and upon being privately and separately examined by me, did declare that she does freely, voluntarily, and without any compulsion, dread or fear of any person or persons whomsoever, renounce, release, and forever relinquish unto the within named grantee,

heirs and assigns, all her interest and estate, and also all her right and claim of Dower, of, in or to all and singular the premises within mentioned and released.

GIVEN under my hand and seal, this day of , Anno Domini 19

(L. S.)
Notary Public for S. C.

(L. S.)

I hereby certify that the within deed has been this day of , A. D. 19
Recorded in Book of Deeds, Page
Fee $
Auditor for Horry County, S. C.

Recorded this 1st day of August A. D. 1941, in Book I Page 234, Fee $
H. B. Brown
Auditor for Horry County, S. C.

Viola Bell sold the second tract of 49 acres to Tyson on July 8, 1941. It sold for $600 plus a mortgage. It was named Pearl Beach after her daughter Ila Pearl, who witnessed the transaction as the notary public at 23. Tyson's total of 96 acres was four blocks. (Horry County Deeds.)

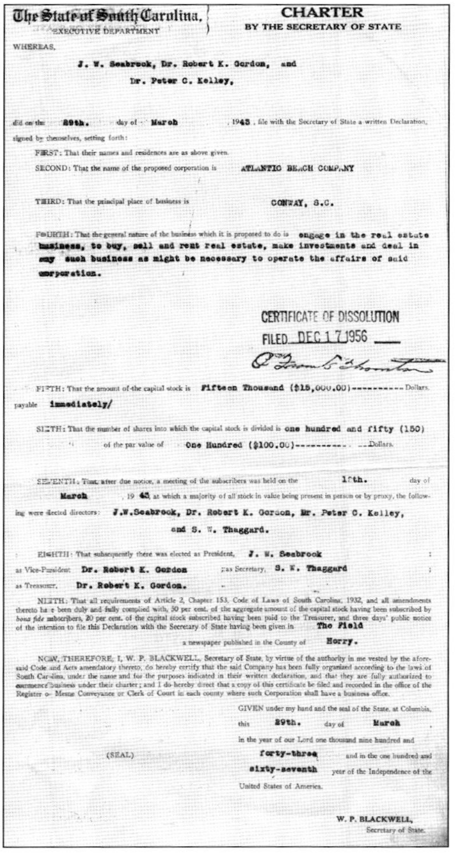

The State of South Carolina,
EXECUTIVE DEPARTMENT

CHARTER
BY THE SECRETARY OF STATE

WHEREAS,

J. W. Seabrook, Dr. Robert K. Gordon, and Dr. Peter C. Kelley,

did on the 29th. day of March, 1943, file with the Secretary of State a written Declaration, signed by themselves, setting forth:

FIRST: That their names and residences are as above given.

SECOND: That the name of the proposed corporation is ATLANTIC BEACH COMPANY

THIRD: That the principal place of business is CONWAY, S.C.

FOURTH: That the general nature of the business which it is proposed to do is engage in the real estate business, to buy, sell and rent real estate, make investments and deal in any such business as might be necessary to operate the affairs of said corporation.

CERTIFICATE OF DISSOLUTION
FILED DEC 17 1956

FIFTH: That the amount of the capital stock is Fifteen Thousand ($15,000.00) Dollars, payable immediately/

SIXTH: That the number of shares into which the capital stock is divided is one hundred and fifty (150) of the par value of One Hundred ($100.00) Dollars.

SEVENTH: That after due notice, a meeting of the subscribers was held on the 1?th. day of March, 19 43, at which a majority of all stock in value being present in person or by proxy, the following were elected directors: J.W.Seabrook, Dr. Robert K. Gordon, Mr. Peter C. Kelley, and S. W. Thaggard.

EIGHTH: That subsequently there was elected as President, J. W. Seabrook; as Vice-President Dr. Robert K. Gordon; as Secretary, S. W. Thaggard; as Treasurer, Dr. Robert K. Gordon.

NINTH: That all requirements of Article 2, Chapter 153, Code of Laws of South Carolina, 1932, and all amendments thereto have been duly and fully complied with, 50 per cent. of the aggregate amount of the capital stock having been subscribed by *bona fide* subscribers, 20 per cent. of the capital stock subscribed having been paid to the Treasurer, and three days' public notice of the intention to file this Declaration with the Secretary of State having been given in The Field a newspaper published in the County of Horry.

NOW, THEREFORE, I, W. P. BLACKWELL, Secretary of State, by virtue of the authority in me vested by the aforesaid Code and Acts amendatory thereto, do hereby certify that the said Company has been fully organized according to the laws of South Carolina, under the name and for the purposes indicated in their written declaration, and that they are fully authorized to commence business under their charter; and I do hereby direct that a copy of this certificate be filed and recorded in the office of the Register of Mesne Conveyance or Clerk of Court in each county where such Corporation shall have a business office.

GIVEN under my hand and the seal of the State, at Columbia, this 29th. day of March, in the year of our Lord one thousand nine hundred and forty-three and in the one hundred and sixty-seventh year of the Independence of the United States of America.

(SEAL)

W. P. BLACKWELL,
Secretary of State.

Drs. Seabrook, Gordon, and Kelly (sometimes spelled "Kelley") signed the Atlantic Beach Company charter. Seabrook was president of Fayetteville State Teachers College (now Fayetteville State University) from 1933 to 1956. He was president of the Atlantic Beach Company from 1943 to 1956. He and his wife, Dr. Mae Hatchette, Ph.D., had one daughter. Dr. Gertha Gibson (1928–2000), Atlantic Beach landowner and historian, wrote about Seabrook in her University of North Carolina dissertation, completed in 1987 and housed at Fayetteville State University. (South Carolina Secretary of State's Office.)

The Pee Dee Medical Association held its annual meeting at the Gordon Hotel with a reception at the Atlantic Beach home of Dr. and Mrs. Robert K. Gordon. The Gordon extended family and friends, shown in the early 1950s at the Gordon home, included the following, pictured from left to right: (seated on the ground) two unidentified, Dr. B. T. Williams, James Kingsland (center at the feet of his grandmother, Mrs. Gordon), Mrs. H. H. Cooper Sr. (Ada Sawyer), Dr. Thomas Miller (third from right), Anna Mae Dixon, Mrs. Thomas Miller; (second row) three unidentified, Mrs. B. T. Williams, Mrs. R. K. Gordon (Mayme Sawyer), three unidentified, Mrs. Harold Kelly, unidentified; (third row) three unidentified, Dr. Wilson, four unidentified, Dr. H. H. Cooper Jr., Dr. Robert K. Gordon, and unidentified; (fourth row) Mrs. Wilson, unidentified, and Dr. Harold Kelly, M.D. (Dr. H. H. Cooper Jr.)

This is a rear view of the H. H. Cooper oceanfront home. (Cooper.)

Seated are Dr. H. H. Cooper Sr. and his wife, Ada Sawyer Cooper. Standing from left to right are their sons Drs. H. H. Jr., Noble, and Edward Cooper. They were the only family to rebuild on the oceanfront in 1955, the year after Hurricane Hazel, until the late 1990s (when Dr. Williams and Ms. McNeill built their homes). (Cooper.)

This 1940s photograph of the H. H. Cooper Sr. home shows the front ocean view in the path of destruction that hit Myrtle Beach on October 15, 1954. Myrtle Beach recovered and thrived within six months, said Dianne DeVaughn and Chuck Stokes in their video for the hurricane's 50th anniversary. (Cooper.)

Lorraine Humphries (soon to be married to Yaro Stropnicky), as a single white female at Myrtle Beach in 1936, would typically have kept black men from straying across the line for fear of their lives, literally. South Carolina had the ninth-highest number of lynchings between 1882 and 1968: 160 out of 4,743 across the country, according to *Lynching Statistics by State*, Archives at Tuskegee Institute. (Fay Porter.)

Lorraine and Yaro Stropnicky were a young white couple vacationing on July 4, 1936, in Myrtle Beach. Lorraine died after 63 years with Yaro. Fay Porter, who fell in love with Yaro when she was eight years old, finally got to marry him, but he died three months later. (Porter.)

Lorraine Stropnicky is pictured at a family outing at the then whites-only Myrtle Beach. A road opened from Conway in 1929, the Grand Forest Hotel was built in 1930, and Myrtle Beach incorporated in 1938. Burroughs and Chapin formed to create the Grand Strand resort out of 77,000 acres that two Burroughs brothers owned, with New York financing. (Porter.)

This could be the "orange rope" in the water that many Atlantic Beach vacationers recall was there to separate blacks from whites. Racial segregation, says *Encyclopedia Britannica*, is "the practice of restricting people to certain circumscribed areas of residence or to separate institutions and facilities on the basis of race." There was more de facto (by custom) than de jure (by law), or Jim Crow, segregation in the Myrtle Beach area. Laws restricted schools. (Porter.)

Bernice McAlister Johnson (1906–2002) of Starr, South Carolina, married William Peter (W. P.) Johnson in 1935, and they had five children—three daughters and two sons. "B. M." was a "phenomenal teacher," according to all of her students, colleagues—everybody she worked with, says daughter Willa. She became the Horry County social studies supervisor. One of 11 children, Johnson received a bachelor's degree from Benedict and a master's degree from South Carolina State College. She was president of the Kingston Lake Women's Baptist Educational and Missionary Convention at Cherry Hill Church. (William Peter Johnson Jr.)

W. P. Johnson's son Charles (left) was an Horry County magistrate, and Pete Jr. (right) was a medically retired major from the U.S. Army and was Atlantic Beach's first town administrator and first town manager. Johnson Sr. bought land because it "gave you a place to go. It wasn't equal to white areas, but it was the best they could do. Before Atlantic Beach itself, black people had no place to go . . . Had to go in the woods." The Johnsons are among the largest landowners on the beach. (Johnson.)

There were three Johnson daughters: Willa, a Ph.D. in education and retired assistant superintendent of Horry County Schools, married Franklin DeWitt, Atlantic Beach's first attorney; Mary Alice, a medical doctor, practices in Washington, D.C.; and Frankie (shown) is a professor of zoology at Michigan State University. (Johnson.)

William Peter Johnson Sr. (1910–2007) bought Tyson land in the 1940s. Born in Lincoln, Georgia, the only child of Frank and Mary Delicious became a distinguished teacher and principal in Horry County Schools after receiving a bachelor's degree in teaching from South Carolina State College. Employment with the U.S. Agriculture Department made W. P. a household name statewide for his local "colored" 4-H clubs and teaching farmers productive techniques. (Johnson.)

Jerry Carmichael (1915–1965) stands on the sand dunes in the 1940s. Though he only finished the seventh grade, he was an avid reader. Carmichael worked as a chef at the PeeDee Lodge in Nichols, as a shipyard stevedore in Wilmington where daughter Dorothy was born, and as a Pullman train cleaner in Baltimore when she was three. He came to Atlantic Beach frequently, often trying to get frightened five-year-old Dorothy into the ocean. (Dorothy Floyd.)

Swimming was a real treat for many visitors who might have come from big cities of the North or even from nearby rural areas. Some remember the orange rope that separated them from the white section of the ocean, but no matter—"we knew where we belonged," states Pete Johnson Jr. Hurricane damage, of course, closes down the beach for a time. (Rosa Stanley.)

Stephanie Simmons and daughter Latifiah enjoy a dip in segregated waters. Alice Graham states in an ABHS interview, "I cannot understand how they thought if we were in water confined to one spot that they wouldn't be contaminated by our blackness [laughs] just because they put up a rope. It's water and it's flowing. It makes no sense." (Stanley.)

Rosa Stanley enjoyed swimming with granddaughter Latifiah. Rosa and her four children, Stephanie, Charles, Luvenia, and Pamela (in Virginia), are the few who can call Atlantic Beach home, having been born, attended schools, and most of them still living here. (Stanley.)

Fishing off the pier, off the shore, and off a boat were favorite pastimes. Right along with the men daily was Rosa Stanley's aunt Lula Jarrott (pictured seated in center, with cap on). Aunt Lula was the daughter of Janie and John Roland Williams and was born in Green Sea. At an early age, she became a member of the First Missionary Baptist Church and was a member of the Mystic Order of Golden Eagles. (Stanley.)

Young Charles Simmons eyes this large fish catch with his mother, Rosa Stanley, her brother-in-law Nate Stanley, and Ike Simmons, who later became one of the town's several police chiefs. "Fishing had triple importance: dietary, economic, and social. Spot is the most abundant, easiest to catch, and best-tasting saltwater pan fish," said Randall A. Wells in *Swamp, Strand & Steamboat*. (Stanley.)

Crescent Beach, called Atlantic Beach pier by its locals, was wiped out by Hurricane Hugo in 1989. Randall Wells wrote, "Like tobacco growing, seining was typically communal. Schools of mullet and spot 'ran' southward in the autumn, and people brought long nets (seines) and worked together to catch the fish." (Stanley.)

This photograph of four men with fishing net, also on the cover, captures one aspect of Atlantic Beach as once a place of peace and productivity that continues somewhat today. The October Fish Fry drew (but now only by special request) many residents and visitors for open-air cooking around large black kettles full of piping hot oil. They would sample sweet potatoes (yams) shaped like home fried potatoes, cole slaw, and a spot "fish sammich." (Lewis.)

Rosa Stanley stands proud, though swimmers—black and white—stopped coming en masse to Atlantic Beach with integration. Due to the lack of oceanfront development, this is the most pristine place to sun, swim, walk (though just four blocks), and fish. Also, there are few places along the Grand Strand, or most anywhere else, that afford a full view of the water all the way from the highway two long blocks westward. (Stanley.)

Friends of Lorraine and Yaro Stropnicky from 1936 represent the four white communities that combined into North Myrtle Beach in 1968, leaving a white majority community on either side of Atlantic Beach. Their now renounced incorporation dates had been as follows: Ocean Drive (1948), Crescent Beach (1953), Cherry Grove (1959), and Windy Hill (1964). Myrtle Beach had been incorporated since 1938. Atlantic Beach incorporated in 1966. (Porter.)

Rosa Stanley, John Sketers, and others pose outside of First Missionary Baptist Church, built in 1947. Rev. Luther Graham (1949–1973), Rev. Luther Small (1974–1982), and Rev. Solon J. Chestnut (1989–2001) were the longest serving pastors. One long-tenured member was Millard Rucker Sr., Sunday school superintendent and treasurer (from 1947 to 1991). (Stanley.)

These men may be coming from a funeral. In 1950, the Ku Klux Klan drove through in a large caravan headed to Charlie Fitzgerald's dance hall in Myrtle Beach. They cut off Charlie's ears, and one of their own was killed, according to Horace Carter in *Views of Fear*. "Atlantic Beach men were armed and ready to defend themselves," remembers Emma Lee Vereen. The man in the center is identified by Rosa Stanley as a Mr. Scott, with the Atlantic Beach police force. (Stanley.)

Stephanie Simmons is pictured on a pony in front of W. K. Smith's motel. For fun today, children rely on the community center, church, and their parents—most of whom live in the Public Housing Authority: Barbara Ann, Cecilia, Keisha Black; Tracy Perkins (Plantation House), Jennifer Bennett (four, including twins); Wanda Parker Chapman (one daughter in Iraq, teen mom home), Tracy Bellamy; and two sons (29th); Freda Baker (three); Anna Edwards (three); and Ora Ladson (two). (Stanley.)

Stephanie Simmons's 10-year-old birthday party was a cookout at the home of Mary Glass on Thirty-first Avenue. Today there are many "foreign" family celebrations with Spanish tunes and Moroccan aromas in the air. Alexia with her two sons (Ladd and Lon) and daughters (Lillie and Lois Sanchez—not their real names) are protective of their immigrant status yet very involved in school and community. Mohammad, Laila Alami-Sounni, their American-born daughter Fadwa, and two sons Yassin and Anas have proudly lived here 13 years. (Stanley.)

Like the Public Housing Authority parents, many of those who live in the disability units there also help watch over the children in the community: Gary Bell, president, Housing Authority Board; Barbara Bellamy; Hattie and Leon Anthony; Frances Parker; Margaret Johnson; and the late Ann Williams and her sister Marian. (Stanley.)

Stephanie Simmons's party was under "The Tree." Many years later, Ben C. Boozer, then executive director of the South Carolina Downtown Development Association, on an economic development cause, "expected to find a community the world had passed by; instead he found a lot of . . . fierce proprietary pride in the community's heritage." Today this remains a gathering place for some and a "home" for Papa Smurf (whose real name is John Wesley McGill) and Willie Keel. It is next to the Eva and Carl McMillan property behind town hall on Thirty-first Avenue. (Stanley.)

Mary Harley Glass Williams (1914–1997) was one of the first women to operate a business in Atlantic Beach—the Silver Platter, where Simmons's birthday party was held. She was the second female to serve on the town council (1973–1978). She was the Mother of the Church at First Baptist Missionary. She hosted cookouts Easter Sunday and First Sundays. Mary Glass's neighbor Ada Graham has lived on Highway 17 for decades, observing it all. (Stanley.)

The Gibson girls (the three daughters of Gertha Smith and John Thomas) grew up in a "tranquil and idyllic" Atlantic Beach, as they remembered it. There was no family business to live with and operate—just an ocean boulevard and knotty pine wood house. Robertha Peyton Gibson is an attorney; Valda Gibson, a doctor; and Denise Gibson Bailey, a church administrator. (Stanley.)

Hubert Williams Jr., whose father bought land from George W. Tyson, warns that had child labor laws been enforced, many five- and six-year-olds like him would have been put out of business selling snow cones and earning hundreds of dollars for the family. (Stanley.)

Rosa Stanley, holding Carolyn Floyd (her mother's adopted charge) with an unidentified man, recalls a favorite church spiritual sung at First Missionary Baptist Church: "Who is gonna tell the child about Jesus? Who is gonna tell the child about God? I really do believe it's my responsibility to tell the child about Jesus. I really do believe it's my responsibility to tell the child about God." Rosa and her friend LaRue Sherman are raising her grandson, Marcus Graham. (Stanley.)

W. K. Smith owned this motel on the corner of Ocean Drive and Thirtieth Avenue (Front Street). While Smith's Place is no longer there, the motel and apartments of today are still small and modestly furnished. A paper curtain may separate the shower stall from a cinder-block bedroom, with thin sheet, cover, and double bed—no television, no refrigerator or stove, no iron or board, no microwave or computer connection. (Curt Teich Archives.)

Hotel Marshall, built in 1945, has survived four hurricanes—Hazel, Hugo, Floyd, and Charley—but the damage is evident. There were sleeping rooms, parlors, ice cream, and swimsuit rentals, according to current owner Brenda Rowell-Bromell. For 20 years, it operated as the Boss nightclub—the name still shows. Susan Hoffer McMillan first displayed this image in *Myrtle Beach and Conway in Vintage Postcards* (Arcadia Publishing). (Curt Teich Archives.)

The back of this postcard reads, "This is Hotel Gordon, the famous beach front hotel at Atlantic Beach, SC. With hot and cold water in every room, with private or semi-private bath, Beautyrest mattresses, and a spacious dining room, offering food second to none. OPEN THE YEAR ROUND." Cora Hodge Taylor, an active property owner with her husband, Charles, remembered the Gordon domicile as a "mansion," with maid's quarters in back. Cora's parents built a Second Street 1940s two-story white structure that withstood Hurricane Hazel but was remodeled after a fire. (Cooper.)

Leugenia Walker Marshall stands: "Peoples passed, pullin' in here. No you can't stop here, this a black beach, for black people. 'We seed the sign.' Wasn't no signs, wasn't no whites. Didn't need that. We just havin' a big time. But the life of my husband. Was the worse thing, being here. God left me. Ninety-five years old, now, and he allowed me back in the Hotel Marshall." Charleston artist Arianne King Comer painted fancy folks there. (Brenda Rowell-Bromell.)

This Jim Lewis design resembles his Parkview Motel across the street. From the 1940s into the 1970s, these "pillars" literally built Atlantic Beach: Jim Lewis, Lefuel Sketers, Eugene Woods, Lenon Evans, Ransom Rowell, P. D. Mitchell, Frank Isom, the Murrays, the Parmleys, W. K. Smith, Emery Gore, Thelton Gore, W. H. and W. V. Gore, Millard Rucker, Thaxton Dixon, J. B. DeWitt, and "Punk" Daniels. Some had visited since the 1940s; some moved in as residents. (Lewis.)

J&L Motel was the first on Front Street (Thirtieth Avenue) after oceanfront buildings. There was another one up the street called L&J, named after the builder and his wife—Jim and Lucille Lewis. These establishments and others provided jobs and lodging. (Lewis.)

This Jim Lewis home design, like other buildings he created, caught on with others. Emma Lee Vereen remarked, "Jim Lewis—very prosperous person. Outspoken. Liked to take a chance. Not afraid to say what he thought. Erected a lot of buildings. Hotels, the big arcade, first; pool tables, Machines, behind where Crazy Horse, behind Russell Skeeters's place and all houses around his house." (Lewis.)

The first carry-out restaurant in Atlantic Beach to serve the crowd on the move, at a time when blacks were served at the rear in whites-only places, was another Jim Lewis contribution. Like the other pillars of the community—so named by their offspring and observers—Lewis was highly thought of and most prolific in his building endeavors. C. Burgin "C. B." Berry, famed land surveyor from Crescent Beach, took over from A. J. Baker in doing the staking and mapping for all the Atlantic Beach landowners. (Lewis.)

James "Jim" Lewis (1915–2000), here relaxing on a sofa, married Lucille (1919–2002) and bought land in the 1950s. They were blessed with three children—James Lenwood Lewis, Otis Tisdale, and Carmeal Miller. The Lewises built numerous apartment complexes in addition to several motels. (Lewis.)

Esau Jenkins (1929–1972), a businessman and civil rights leader, was born on Johns Island near Charleston, South Carolina. He and his wife, Janie Jones Jenkins, had seven children. "My father purchased his place at Atlantic Beach in 1948. The lot was 150 feet by 300 feet. The land cost $500–$600. He borrowed the money from people because he could not get it from the bank." (Avery Research Center.)

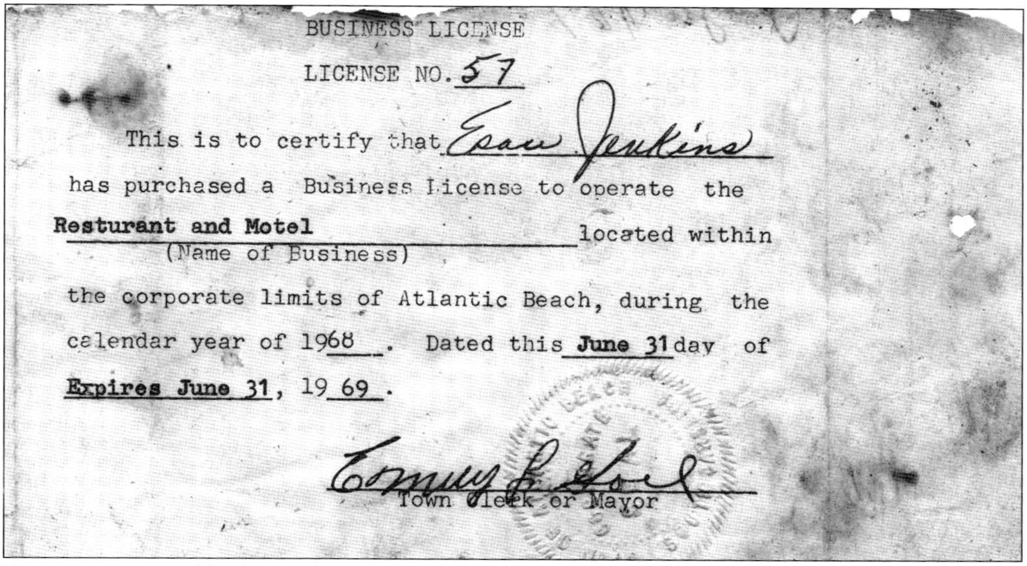

BUSINESS LICENSE

LICENSE NO. 57

This is to certify that Esau Jenkins has purchased a Business License to operate the Resturant and Motel (Name of Business) located within the corporate limits of Atlantic Beach, during the calendar year of 1968. Dated this June 31 day of

Expires June 31, 1969.

Emery L. Gore
Town Clerk or Mayor

Former mayor and building inspector Emery Gore signed this permit. Abraham Jenkins, Esau's eldest son, told Veronica Gerald, "He built a little restaurant with a kitchen, table and on the back was a place to sleep. He also rented six rooms on the back. He later built a 10-room motel. It was called E. Jenkins Place." Esau Jenkins, a "lieutenant" (second in command in Charleston during the civil rights movement) to Rev. Dr. Martin Luther King Jr., convened whites and blacks there. (ABHS, Preserving Memories, Avery.)

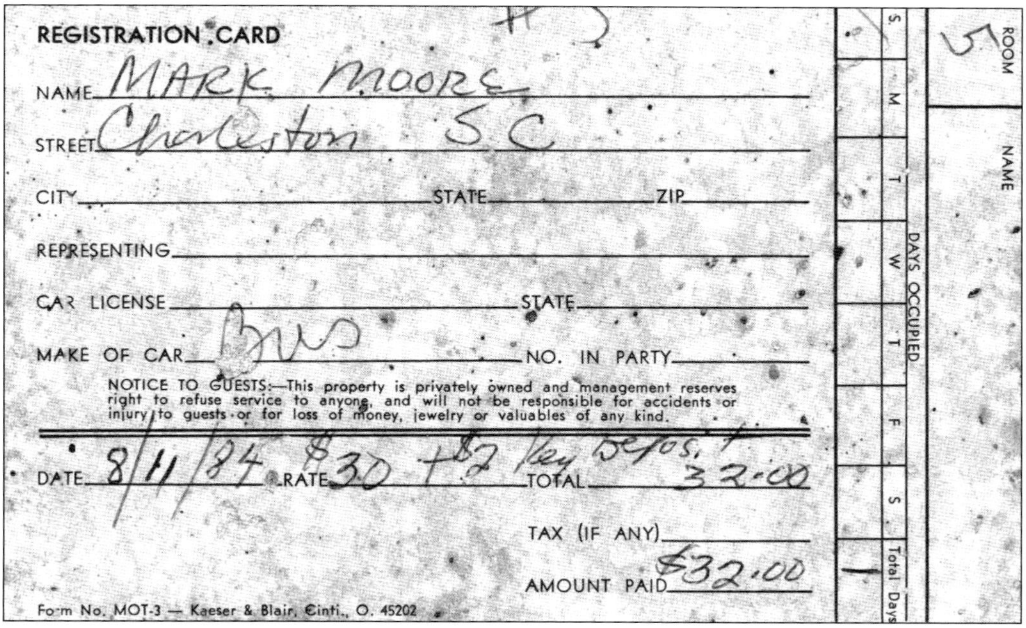

REGISTRATION CARD

NAME MARK MOORE

STREET Charleston S.C

CITY ___ STATE ___ ZIP ___

REPRESENTING ___

CAR LICENSE ___ STATE ___

MAKE OF CAR Bus NO. IN PARTY ___

NOTICE TO GUESTS:—This property is privately owned and management reserves right to refuse service to anyone, and will not be responsible for accidents or injury to guests or for loss of money, jewelry or valuables of any kind.

DATE 8/11/84 RATE $30 + $2 key Depos. TOTAL 32.00

TAX (IF ANY) ___

AMOUNT PAID $32.00

ROOM 5 | NAME

DAYS OCCUPIED: S M T W T F S Total Days

Form No. MOT-3 — Kaeser & Blair, Cinti., O. 45202

The Jenkins motel registration reminds, "During the late 40s and 50s, Atlantic Beach used to be so packed people couldn't find any place to stay. Everybody who had something on the beach would be sold out. There were never enough places. Many places rented by the hour to be used as a place to get cleaned up." Jenkins's offspring are lawyers, architects, planners, and so on. (ABHS, Preserving Memories, Avery.)

"If you build it they will come." This couple and two girls in front of a car are just some of the hordes of folks who came to the beach from Florida; Georgia; North and South Carolina; New York; New Jersey; Maryland; Washington, D.C.; Virginia; Connecticut; and Massachusetts. There were other black beaches, but many people preferred Atlantic Beach. (Stanley.)

The www.SoulofAmerica.com Web site lists the following as historically black beaches that survive today: American Beach, Florida; Atlantic Beach, South Carolina; Butler Beach, Florida; Bethune-Volusia Beach, Florida; and Highland Beach, Maryland. Only Atlantic and Highland are known to be black-owned and governed. Sandy Island, federally reserved now, is a little-known black oasis accessible only by boat near Brookgreen Gardens, south of Myrtle Beach. (Stanley.)

Robert Hayes was a cook from Ocean Drive. Others came to Atlantic Beach from up and down the East Coast from April to October, 24 hours a day, seven days a week. (Stanley.)

Wilbert Miles ("Tutey"), a waiter at Early's Restaurant in Windy Hill, came to Atlantic Beach from Charleston. As mentioned on the Web site of the College of Charleston's Avery Research Center for African American History and Culture, Charleston's Mosquito Beach, located off of James Island, "was a popular recreation spot for Lowcountry African Americans, unable to use the area's segregated beaches. Over time, a thriving boardwalk and 'juke joint' developed there." (Stanley.)

This lady might have visited McKenzie Beach, located between Pawley's Island and Murrell's Inlet. Less commercial than other black beaches, McKenzie was just a family recreational outlet for vacationers drawn from Georgetown and Myrtle Beach. Now owners and visitors come from New York, Canada, and New England. A few black faces show the gentrification of McKenzie. The author finds these ruins haunting. The source is www.cofc.edu/avery. (Stanley.)

This is baby Luvenia Stanley. Hilton Head and Daufuskie Island used to be all-black safe havens for vacationers and residents alike. Development has reversed the percentages "from 100 percent to barely 10 percent [blacks]," one tour guide responded to an inquiry. "English sea captain William Hilton first took over this new land from the Spanish-speaking Indians in 1663 and held it until after the Civil War, when blacks preserved it," as documented at www.hiltonheadisland.com. (Stanley.)

Rosa Stanley, pictured in front of a car at Tony's, reminds people that even Myrtle Beach's oceanfront land was once owned by black people for years until they were recently (in the 1980s) pushed back into streets significantly named Carver, Dunbar, and Martin Luther King Jr. Just a short four to five blocks westward, the problems in middle-class neighborhoods are now in full view of the opulent Radisson Hotel and Myrtle Beach Convention Center. (Stanley.)

Lorraine Stropnicky represents the story told by A. E. Jordan Jr. The father of A. E. Jordan Sr., Isaiah "I. C." Cleveland, bought the strip of land in the 1940s known as "the segregation ditch." A mound of dirt on the Windy Hill oceanfront and a fence at Bay Watch (the old Holiday Inn) keep the town segregated now by choice of current black Atlantic Beach residents, rather than by intention of white neighboring communities. (Porter.)

Winter sometimes comes to the beach, as demonstrated by these ladies in coats. It even snows on occasion! In front of the Big Apple, from left to right, are Mary Randall Edge, or "Peaches" (1932–2009), who lived in the Neck (Little River) and used to help the Evans and Watson businesses; Emma Lee Vereen; and Sally, who was Flora Watson's (Mable's) niece. Mary's brother is Bishop Charles Randall, pastor of St. Delight Holiness Church in Little River, South Carolina. He was twice a candidate for statehouse. (Stanley.)

On the other hand, this unidentified lady in a Jim Lewis picture demonstrates a fashionable summer frock. In future studies for the town's development, including the Keenan Plan, it is the Caribbean theme that keeps coming up, with jazz and African motifs in building construction and for interior physical entertainment venues. (Lewis.)

Two

Heyday

Buses, Bikers, Dining, and Dancing to R&B Music

Motel proprietor Mable Daniels Powell (left) and an unidentified cousin stand next to the Holiday Motel sign. This cornerstone facility stayed in service right until its demolition in 2006. (Mildred Daniels McKoy.)

Holiday Motel was built in 1960 by "the first black female entrepreneur on the Grand Strand," reads Mable Daniels Powell's obituary. This oceanfront lodging accommodated many of Atlantic Beach's visitors. Pictured is owner Mable Daniels Powell, cousin Angelo ? Jr., and Powell's daughter "little Mable." (Daniels.)

The Holiday Motel had 46 rooms, balconies, and a 50-seat dining room. It stood adjacent to the Holiday Inn chain, in North Myrtle Beach, and held its own. The two-story structure had two wings, one running parallel to the ocean and the other perpendicular. A courtyard in the middle provided ample space for parking, turnarounds, and tour bus drop-offs. (Daniels.)

Mable Daniels Powell (1908–1995) shows off a Christmas gift in front of the tree. Powell was born, lived, and died in Whiteville, North Carolina. Her union to the late Phillip Daniels Jr. produced four children, one of whom, Samuel Daniels, predeceased her; the other children were the late Wilbert ("Punk's Patio") Daniels, Mable Daniels, and Mildred Daniels McKoy. The Daniels family stayed in the Holiday Motel during the beach season, though, like 90 percent of Atlantic Beach, are absentee landowners. (Daniels.)

According to her obituary, Mable Daniels Powell (who remarried James Wallace Powell after Phillip Daniels died) was also "the only black female proprietor on the Grand Strand's Atlantic Beach, South Carolina." She is pictured standing at the motel door entrance. (Daniels.)

Mable Daniels Powell and members of her kitchen crew pose dressed in starch-white uniforms, prepared to serve the multitudes that flocked to the Holiday Motel. (Daniels.)

An unidentified diner at the Holiday Motel stands out among many who were attending the North Carolina Mutual meeting on July 20, 1978. The Holiday Motel specialized in seafood platters: lobster, crab, and shrimp. (Daniels.)

On the right is famed blues singer Big Joe Turner (1911–1985). Turner's hits included "Corrine, Corrina," the original "Shake, Rattle and Roll," and "Honey Hush." On the left is Turner's unidentified road manager. Dot Floyd says, "We used to drive down from Nichols, South Carolina, with my 13-year-old cousin behind the wheel. We would spend the day then return to his house before night fall in order to let the grown-ups drive down for the evening. My family spent summers in Nichols in the 1940s coming from Baltimore. We had lots of fun in Atlantic Beach—both children and adults." (Daniels.)

Mildred Daniels McKoy is serving a guy at the bar. "People would drink all day up there so they would be looking tore down coming back like they was going up," remembers Jerome Yeardon from Charleston. (Daniels.)

Wilbert Edward "Punk" Daniels (1926–1997), bedecked with straw hat and cigarette drooping, greets guests in the Holiday Motel dining room. The son of the late Phillip Daniels Jr. and Mable Daniels Powell, "Punk" graduated from Whiteville Negro School, attended Southeastern Community College, and was honorably discharged from the U.S. Armed Forces. (Daniels.)

In the center, underneath the "Big Daddy" sign, stands "Punk" Daniels and some "Punk's Patio" patrons. Daniels used to have another patio where the old Solid Gold was on Front Street. He was an entrepreneur for 40 years, taking over from his departed mother the Goodwill Funeral Home. He was a member of the Masonic Hall of Hannah Lodge 3204 of Hallsboro, North Carolina. He and his wife, Bertha E. Yates, united a family of one girl, Jacqueline, a son, Tony Curtis, and a foster son, Dickie L. Hickman. (Daniels.)

Mable Daniels Powell, front center, greets this tour bus group with Holiday Motel cheer. Her daughter Mildred was a schoolteacher in Whiteville. Atlantic Beach had its own gas station, W. V. Gore ESSON, on Highway 17 where Lady J's sits, still black owned (Daniels.)

"But that used to be a lot of fun—taking those bus trips. Everybody would get so drunk, the adults," Jerome Yeardon recalls. "Once somebody took a case of Wild Irish. One or two bottles of Wild Irish is okay, but if you abuse it. . . . Like a case. People started looking tore down by the time the bus arrived." (Daniels.)

Children arrive at the beach by bus. "Atlantic Beach was a wonderful area for children," Willie Isom told the ABHS. "Look at this wall [of children's pictures]. I told you their accomplishments. I'm proud of what Atlantic Beach offered us, 'cause if we didn't stay on Atlantic Beach, we couldn't afford to send our children to school." Sunday school outings brought them by the hundreds. (Daniels.)

"Dozier's Rabbit Box sold cookies, hot dogs, hamburgers," said Etrulia Dozier, a retired librarian from Whittemore in Conway. "Both my husband and I taught during the school season, so that it was a way for us to have a really good time. . . . Just watching other people come down from wherever they came from, to enjoy the beach and, a lot of people came to the beach." (Daniels.)

More Holiday Motel guests in the courtyard are in front of cars and on the balcony. "Some motels rented on a 12-hour basis to accommodate the demand," explained Dot Floyd. There was "nothing around for miles and miles, it seemed that Atlantic Beach was much bigger than just four blocks. Nothing was developed at the time and there was just woods and farmland." (Daniels.)

This large crowd is leaving the Holiday Motel headed for the streets of Atlantic Beach to enjoy the sights, sounds, and sensations. Brenda Rowell-Bromell cites other lodgings: R. Rowell Hotel and Grocery, Gordon Hotel, Palms Motel, Gateway Inn, Scotteretta Motel, Superfine Motel, Mr. Smith's Place, and, of course, Hotel Marshall. (Daniels.)

"Atlantic Beach was blooming in those days because Black people came from all around. There had been a lot of black folk that had gone North because of employment and when they came back to Horry County to visit their relatives, Atlantic Beach was the place they wanted to go. . . . they were going to Atlantic Beach to have a good time," Etrulia Dozier explained to the Atlantic Beach Historical Society. With her late husband, Gibb, educator and World War II veteran, she owned three lots and ran a little hot dog stand in the 1950s. (Daniels.)

"And then, sometimes a bus would be on the side of the road and the other buses would pass it up with people on the bus waving 'See Ya!' to those left behind," Jerome Yeardon chuckles. (Daniels.)

There were many places to go—some now-famous musicians were there to stay and perform. Baby Grand Restaurant, Idle Hour, Buster Brown's place, Corner Bar and Grill, Cotton Club, Mary Glass's place, and Punk's Patio were some of the places. "Chubby Checker stayed at Esau Jenkins", Earlene Woods tells. The Tams stayed at Evans Motel: "We loved Earlene, Irene [the daughter], and the first Mrs. Woods," recalls Diane Pope, The Tams' manager. "Little Richard bought a hearse from Mr. Rucker to haul his equipment, and stayed in my hotel, the Blue Bird Inn," said Willie Isom. Mildred Daniels McKoy adds that Little Richard stayed at their Holiday Motel, too, as did Tommy Edwards, who gave Mildred's mother a big gold watch. (Daniels.)

"People would ride up there with a girlfriend and come back alone or with somebody else. They had so many buses from Charleston, everywhere. People forgot which one they came on. As long as there was a seat and it was going to Charleston [or wherever], people would hop on," Jerome Yeardon recounts. (Daniels.)

Black bikers were coming to the beach in the 1960s and 1970s, long before the now-famous BikeFest, which is approaching its 30th anniversary in 2010. Many rode the larger, more expensive Harley-Davidson bikes, but the majority rode Japanese brands like Kawasaki, Suzuki, Honda, and Yamaha. This distinguished, along with race, the difference between the Myrtle Beach Harley Spring Rally mid-May and the Atlantic Beach BikeFest at the end of May, Memorial Day weekend. (Daniels.)

The first Atlantic Beach rally with parade floats and biker contests was in 1980 and grew from an initial 100 bikers to the nearly 400,000 tourists still flocking to the Grand Strand stretches from below Garden City at the south end to Atlantic Beach above Little River north, where the Blue Crab Festival is also held in May. (Daniels.)

It has been said that BikeFest was started to raise money for the town. Regrettably, the town never franchised the event or its products, so it never capitalized from it. The lion's share of the revenue went to Myrtle Beach. Black bikers were already going to the Harley-Davidson rally and began to want to host their own rally two weeks later, Memorial Day weekend, so Carolina Knight Riders worked with the town. (Daniels.)

The NAACP urged a successful boycott of South Carolina in 2000 to get the Confederate flag lowered from the state capitol. They successfully sued the Yachtsman Resort and the City of Myrtle Beach in 2005, for discriminating practices. The City of Myrtle Beach has initiated measures to curb both Harley-Davidson's rally and BikeFest. These actions have impacted attendance, but hundreds of thousands still come. (Daniels.)

"Integration [came] gradual—saw the busloads going to Holiday Inn, and down in Myrtle Beach, but still did not know what it meant for Atlantic Beach. Holiday buses came from Charleston and Wilmington. Integration: You could see the buses parked in Myrtle Beach in parking lot. Oh this is where everybody is. Buses got less and less," Emma Lee Vereen reminisces as the crowds wave. The 1960s accommodations laws paved the way for integration, but Atlantic Beach thought the blacks would still return. (Daniels.)

"Buses would leave two, three, four in the morning, all hours through the night," Yeardon tells. "Y'all Come Back, Now" was a familiar Atlantic Beach sendoff that store owner Bernice Rowell still says to departing guests from daughter Brenda's restaurant. (Daniels.)

From 1965, Billy Scott, pictured with his wife at the time, Barbara, and Janet Helm, as the Prophets (sometimes called Georgia, and now Party), has written and performed R&B clasics. In 1985, he was inducted into the R&B Music Hall of Fame and in 1995 he founded the Carolina Beach Music Awards Show (the Cammys). In February 2001, Billy's "My Kind of Girl" went to number one and stayed on the Top 40 R&B chart an uprecedented 20 weeks. Billy Scott told the ABHS, "We would get done with a gig, be dead tired from the bus or car ride down, and go from one motel to the next at midnight or later, looking for a room. Most motels would not even give a reason for the turn down, but would just say no, nothing is available, no vacancy or whatever." (Billy Scott.)

"Then somebody would say something like, 'Have you tried Atlantic Beach? You can probably find a room up there. I am sure they will have a room for you,'" remembers Scott. "Then we would get there and get the red carpet treatment. We were home. The Sketerses, Earlene Woods, The Gores—all of them, would just open the doors, no matter how late at night. Give us clean sheets, towels, food." (Scott.)

Rosa Stanley stands by a "piccolo," or jukebox, in one of the famous Atlantic Beach patios. The name "beach music" (the state music) came from white kids listening to black R&B music on these boxes because it was banned from the radio. Bill Pinkney and the Drifters, the Temptations, James Brown, and more were the music of choice. (Stanley.)

Pictured is Elmoore at Zeno's Place, owned by Vander Moore Gore's brother. "White kids adapted the black dances of the day—the Lindy hop, jitterbug, swing, and called it the shag (S.C. state dance). Atlantic Beach, along with Seabreeze (black) and Carolina Beach in N.C., Charlie's Place in Myrtle Beach are all credited with the cross-pollination of black music and dance," according to articles contributed by Michael Futch; Judy Collins, owner of Judy's House of Oldies in North Myrtle Beach; and Bo Bryan of "SHAG" Foundation Publications (www.949thesurf.com). (Stanley.)

From left to right, Rosa Stanley, Della Holmes, seated owner Mable Watson Edge (1924–1983), and "Punk" Daniels enjoy her Tony's Restaurant. There used to be a two-story building with a patio next door to Ernestine and Troy Sowell's summer home on Front Street that she tore down and rebuilt. Edge, daughter of the late Deacon Charley Watson and Gussie Graham Watson, was born in Loris. She graduated from high school there and attended Morris College in Sumpter. She taught for several years in the county. Mable was predeceased by her husband, Leroy Edge. (Stanley.)

From left to right are an unidentified man in a hat, young Tony Edge, Mark Simmons, Mable Watson Edge, and Henry Moore, former principal of the colored Chestnut School and an Atlantic Beach resident who who lived on Thirty-second Street until his recent death. Moore is presenting young Tony Edge with cash. Mable Edge named her restaurant (formerly a two-story hotel) Tony's after her adopted son. (Stanley.)

This birthday party for Rosa Stanley was at Mable Edge's restaurant. Famed bars and restaurants included Blue Moon Inn, Polka Dot Grill, and Baby Grand, recounts Emma Lee Vereen, who also bragged about how clean everything was kept, with a lot of flowers on their places. Garbage was kept in a deep pit and burned on Monday to get ready for the week. Thelton Gore, owner of a patio, is on the far left. (Stanley.)

Rosa Stanley's aunt Lula Victoria Jarrott (1912–1992) and Jeffro Hart sit in front of the Big Apple, a little club behind Hotel Marshall. Another place in the area was called Scotteretta and was run by "a big fat man from Georgetown," Stanley recalls. The Big Apple had the same setup—piccolo downstairs and rooms upstairs. (Stanley.)

Punk's Patio was the joint, day and night, for dancing, listening to music, drinking, snacking, and meeting people. "Patio" means a semi-outdoor dance floor and bar—Punk's was the most famous. Jeppy McDowell, shag instructor at Fat Harold's in North Myrtle Beach, introduces each lesson with his personal history as one of the summer lifeguards who used to watch the black teens dance what were considered "forbidden moves"—too "lewd and lascivious"—and modify them for white consumption. (Stanley.)

The skyline in the distance shows Mabel Bell, Punk's Patio, and Holiday Motel. *The Shag* (1980) was filmed here. The Irene Taylor family is holding on to that land under great pressure from developers. Daughters Ladsine and Angela D. Taylor and son Byron ("B. J.") were the children of retired schoolteachers L. J. and Irene Taylor and live in North Carolina. Irene Taylor's lot (not pictured) is the last black-owned oceanfront lot at the corner of Thirtieth Avenue. (Stanley.)

This image of Rosa Stanley at age six shows that children on the beach had fun, too, but most children growing up in Atlantic Beach worked hard in their parents' stores, restaurants, motels, even bars. Rosa, now 63, and her daughter Stephanie are accomplished seamstresses. Stephanie is a Board of Elections worker. Rosa is very active in First Missionary Baptist Church, a regular observer of town politics, and deservedly cochairperson of the historical society. (Stanley.)

Polly Macon, Rosa's cousin, was among the few child residents who went to school "in the country" on the bus that picked them up. Most of the local children went to Sunday school at First Missionary Baptist Church and sang in the choir. (Stanley.)

Rosa at 16 shows the beach child as a teen still having fun, even as she made money—selling snow cones and other entrepreneurial pursuits. Some summer earnings helped teens go to college. At age 63, her favorite pursuit is "plunderin'," meaning looking for or doing something in the yard of her Twenty-ninth Avenue house. (Stanley.)

Tubbie, one of the little boys, participated in town events, contests, and parades like Little Miss or Mr. Atlantic Beach. He was raised by Carrie Williams, who had a place on the beach. But many Atlantic Beach children worked hard with their parents in serving the teeming visitors. A former local official described the tough responsibilities of siblings in making beds, cleaning rooms, reconciling the cash register, serving beverages, and more. Today Malik Simpson carries out those duties at E&E. (Stanley.)

Rosa Stanley remembers Katie Powell, her Twenty-ninth Avenue neighbor: "She and her husband, William, both teachers, came down from Whiteville for summers and holidays and finally built a home in 1971. Atlantic Beach stood out [and] wanted to preserve their blackness, black beach. And have their own mayor," she told an ABHS interviewer. (Stanley.)

Rosa remembers Violet Mitchell when she and her husband, P. D., were actively involved, as with her 20-year tenure as chair of the Municipal Election Committee. Following P. D.'s death in 1987, Mitchell served Atlantic Beach First Baptist Church, where she was Mother of the Church and had served as financial secretary, church clerk, and a deaconess. Violet Mitchell was the last surviving sibling of 14 children. (Stanley.)

Florence Brown Fordham (1905–1967) of Scanlonville in Mount Pleasant, South Carolina, is shown here vacationing at Atlantic Beach. She provided domestic assistance to several Charleston families and was highly valued because of her vast knowledge of kosher dietary laws. Florence and her sons, William, George, Peter, and Oscar, enjoyed many visits to Atlantic Beach during her lifetime, writes William's daughter. (Barbara Fordham Collier.)

Gladys was "a worker from North Carolina," where many property owners are from, many of whom are schoolteachers: Ernestine (Troy, ex-military) Sowell from Supply; and from Fayetteville, Diane (Leonard, banker) Hill; Helen and Melvin (principal) Pierce; Rosa Lee Torrey, and Linwood Haith, third generation Christina's mother was a doctor and her father is an attorney. Retired teachers Irene and L. J. Taylor of Lumberton are some of the few blacks who still own oceanfront land, the former Gore pavilion. They have two daughters, Ladsine and Angela D., and a son, Byron J., or "B. J." (Stanley.)

Evalene was a worker on the beach. "Every Thursday was 'Maid's Day,' when white employers would bring their workers to Atlantic Beach for a holiday," according to the *Black Pearl*. And Carrine Rucker laughed when telling ABHS that July 6, not July 4, was celebrated, because everybody had to work on the actual holiday. (Stanley.)

Young Tony Watson Edge looks sharp. Rev. Mary Anne Jackson McIver (1938–2004), daughter of the late Ike and Fannie Cloud Jackson, taught Conway young people and still has a family beach home in Atlantic Beach. McIver received her bachelor's degree from Claflin University and her master's in education from South Carolina State University, and she taught in Horry County public schools for 33 years. "Following in the footsteps of her mother, 'Ma Fannie,' she provided private piano lessons for over 30 years." She was a member of the Zeta Phi Beta Sorority. Her husband, Leslie, an educator and reverend, and three sons, Kenneth, Keith, and Leslie Jr., remain. Leslie McIver Sr. came in second in the 2008 race for mayor of Conway, and Ken works as town manager. (Stanley.)

Rosa Stanley and Johnny Benton snuggle in 1962 at one of the many roadside souvenir photo stands. There were two Gladys-owned businesses to enjoy: Gladys Snack Shop and Motel (Gladys Bethea) and Atlantic Beach Grocery Store (Gladys Murray). Gladys Nichols Bethea (1908–2007), known as "Mama Gladys," graduated from Fayetteville School of Cosmetology and owned Gladys Beauty Shop for over 50 years in Conway. In Atlantic Beach, she owned Gladys Snack Shop. (Stanley.)

This unidentified couple may be in front of the Atlantic Beach store owned by Gladys Lucille Gordon Murray (1910–2007). "Aunt Gladys" was the fourth child of the late Emma Witherspoon and Joseph Gordon and born in Williamsburg County. She ran the Atlantic Beach Grocery Store with her husband, the late John Charles of Greeleyville, whom she married in 1943. Murray earned a bachelor of science degree in education from South Carolina State University and taught school for 36 years. Murray's is now Brown's Inn on Front Street. (Stanley.)

Many "Negro tourists" who came down from Fayetteville to work on the army base in Myrtle Beach could not sleep or recreate there. "Even German POWs, from submarines that attacked ships along the Grand Strand in 1943, slept on the base. Black soldiers were orderlies, housekeepers, and construction workers," according to Catherine Lewis, but had to pitch tents on Thirty-first Avenue and rent rooms for an hour in Atlantic Beach. Earnest Stanley, uncle of M. Sgt. Orton Bellamy, took many souvenir photographs, especially of military visitors. Jim French is pictured here in the U.S. Navy during World War II. (Charleston Chronicle.)

Bernice Rowell (born 1927) tells how her husband built Ranson Rowell's Grocery, acquired in the late 1940s from Jake Bryant, as a two-story, 25-unit motel to which another 27 units were added for a total of 52 units. She and Ranson Rowell, a decorated military man, came from Marion, South Carolina, and raised their four children between the two communities. (Rowell.)

According to the research of Catherine Lewis, at its peak there were 3,400 active duty members and 6,540 civilian employees on the Myrtle Beach base of 100,000 acres. It was the largest Horry County employer and therefore the largest bastion of segregation. In 2004, it became a major residential, recreational, and commercial community called Market Commons. Jim French was one of five blacks to integrate the once all-white bootcamp training center at Great Lakes, Illinois. French frequently writes about Atlantic Beach as editor and publisher of the *Chronicle*. (Charleston Chronicle.)

L. M. Alston is pictured here. Many young men have been killed, not at war but at home. Amidu "Juice" Nallo (1977–2004) was born in Conway to Amidu and Agnes Nallo, of Sierra Leone heritage. He was junior class president at Conway High School and was a National Honor Society member. He belonged to the Accappela Choir and the soccer and football teams. He attended the University of South Carolina, managed the Nallo motels on the beach, and left an eight-month-old daughter when he was killed there. (Rowell.)

Willie James Lewis, father of ABHS secretary Tema Lewis Hill, is seated in this picture. "Sot" is Gullah for "sat," as in "he sot down." Scholars do not agree on the terms Gullah and Geechee, but generally Gullah people are those located in coastal South Carolina, and Geechee people are those who live along the Georgia coast and into Florida, according to www.nps.gov. The following Lewis family pictures are used to explain more Gullah words. Geechee refers to the people, Gullah to the language, says Muima Maat. (Tema Lewis Hill.)

Willie Lewis half stands by a quarter-moon backdrop. "Wot" is Gullah for "What," as in "wot you doing?" "Geechee" has also been used in a derogatory manner to show disdain for an African American from the Lowcountry region. Many Atlantic Beach people deny these roots. (Hill.)

Willie Lewis fully stands by the quarter moon. These "quarter" pictures were very popular. "Gwine" means "going," as in "I gwine home now." As documented on www.nps.gov, "Gullah/Geechee people of today are descendants of enslaved Africans from various ethnic groups of west and central Africa who were brought to the New World and forced to work on the plantations of coastal South Carolina, Georgia, North Carolina, and Florida." (Hill.)

Vance and Tema Vereen are Tema Lewis Hill's grandfather (dad) and grandmother. "Been yuh, Come yuh" means "I have been here (a native); you just came here (a newcomer)." "Because of their geographic protection from outsiders and strong sense of family and community, Gullah/Geechee people maintained a separate creole language and developed distinct culture patterns, which included more of the African cultural tradition than African American population in other parts of the United States" (www.nps.gov). (Hill.)

Dorothy Lewis was mother to Tema, Chandria, Lisa, Glenn, and Wallace. A "sittin' up" is like a wake, in the home, every day and night right up until the funeral. "Gullah/Geechee people are survivors—unique groups of African Americans—who lived near the coast and on barrier islands that were separated from the mainland by creeks, rivers, and marshes" (www.nps.gov). (Hill.)

Maggie Lewis was Dorothy's mother. Some people still walk dirt roads to get to "The Beach." "The isolation of Gullah/Geechee people which began in colonial times in response to tropical fevers later became an isolation of choice. People chose to come back to their homes, their families, their language, and their way of life—a slow-paced life among majestic trees, tidal marshes, and dirt roads traversed by ox and mule carts" (www.nps.gov). (Hill.)

From left to right are Larry Smalls, Sherry Suttles, and Albert "Cat" Gore. The Smalls and Gore families came in from "the country"—from Wampee, Longs, and Poplar—places where small boats, horses, mules, and feet were the primary forms of transportation for years. Thus, within these rural communities, people were able to maintain their language, arts, crafts, religious beliefs, folklore, rituals, and food preferences that are distinctly connected to their West African roots (www.nps.gov). (ABHS.)

Rosa Stanley (left) is pictured with friend LaRue Sherman. "Dey" or "day" in Gullah meant "there" or "they," as in "She go over dey" or "Day gwine over yonder." Coastal development, changing job markets, and population shifts have forced many Gullah/Geechee people to leave their ancestral family lands. The traditional economy of farming, fishing, hunting, and small-scale marketing of subsistence products has been replaced by a suburban and resort service economy (www.nps.gov). (ABHS.)

Little River resident Sondra Ward started a Gullah/Geechee Festival at the Community Center in 2003. For two years, it included African dancing, vendors, Vermelle "Bunny" Rodrigues, and "Queen Quet" Marquetta L. Goodwine. In 2005 and 2006, the Atlantic Beach Historical Society sponsored the event outdoors. Adande African Drum and Dance Company performed at the ABHS-sponsored Gullah/Geechee Festival, thanks to a generous anonymous developer donor. (Margaret B. Moore, Burgess.)

James Lenwood Lewis (left) is seated with an unidentified man and child. Lenwood is a contractor, following in the footsteps of his father, Jim. He is the father of five. Atlantic Beach was included in the Gullah/Geechee Heritage Corridor initiated by Congressman James Clyburn and could become one of three areas to preserve and promote this culture, which at one point was threatened with extinction. Chicken bogue (or bog) is a Gullah rice, chicken, and sausage casserole served in many restaurants and at outdoor functions. (Lewis.)

This unidentified lady might have enjoyed the various church piano playing of Flora Ellen DeVaughn Grantham-Jones (1909–1974), born in Harolds, North Carolina, to the late Peyton and Ida Herring DeVaughn. She graduated from Fayetteville State Normal College and taught public school in both Carolinas until retiring in 1975. She served on the Housing Authority Board and was treasurer for the Concerned Citizens. (Lewis.)

This unidentified young lady might have been a piano student of Grantham's. Past Grand Worthy Association and Matron of the Eastern Star as well as Daughters of Isis member, Grantham had one daughter, Marian D. Anderson Williams, son-in-law John Williams, and beloved godson Rev. Alphonso Scott. Her home was recently torn down. (Lewis.)

Lee Vander (Gore) Bellamy provided some popular phrases that would often be heard around Atlantic Beach. This couple could be called "Married?" When raised as a question, the word in street talk means courting, or living together. (Stanley.)

This couple could be called "Married, really?" That's street talk for when the marriage is legal, with children. One couple who found love and marriage in Atlantic Beach was Eloise and Emery Gore, the first mayor. E&E motel owner Dr. Leo Twiggs, a renowned visual artist and former board member of the Palmetto Trust for Historic Preservation, honeymooned on the beach with his wife, Rosa Johnson. Jannie and Willie Isom met, married, and raised their children in Atlantic Beach. (Stanley.)

Calling someone "a book person" or "bookish" means they're educated or college trained. (Stanley.)

"I'm just a country boy, girl." That means you might not have skills, might not be sophisticated, but you're really smarter than people think. (Stanley.)

These three unidentified men are alive and happy here. Unfortunately, Atlantic Beach has a long history of violence and death, but fortunately, it has not affected tourists. Familiar names like Robert Marshall, Ranson Rowell Jr., Al Scott, and Amidu "Juice" Nallo are a few among the many, some "unknown soldiers," who died or are incarcerated in the crossfire of an urban environment brought to the beach. (Stanley.)

Pictured is an unidentified tourist. *The Black Pearl: The History of Atlantic Beach, South Carolina*, is a booklet produced as a project of Afro-Fest 1994 by Emma Lee Vereen, Earlene Woods, and Ronald Isom (deceased). According to the *Black Pearl*, "the first town police chief was Henry Hemmingway. Crodger Lewis, the first policeman, was hired in 1953 by the Horry County sheriff. He had to provide his own transportation. Buster Brown was also hired in 1953. But before there were any policemen, the people were together, watching each other's children and taking care of each other. There were no problems with drugs or crime." (Stanley.)

This unidentified girl is dressed for success. (Stanley.)

Pictured are the now-closed public housing units on Thirtieth Avenue in the left background and longtime Atlantic Beach Grocery Store (Brown's Inn now) in the foreground, for sale again. Even today, Hubert H. Williams Jr., a second-generation landowner, worries about the safety of the children and adults in a sometimes dangerous environment that has plagued the beach. The recommendation of Leonard Hill, current president of the Atlantic Beach Property Owners Association, and others to implement overhead street cameras has gone unheard. As Housing Authority units are shut down and no new development begins, less and less street activity is occurring. For a time, though, bootlegging and prostitution went hand in hand. Unlike other areas where one could get liquor easily enough, says Pop Sadler, in Atlantic Beach, it was a one-stop shop where whites and blacks alike came for booze, babes, dinner, and dancing. (Stanley.)

As documented in Randall Wells's *Oral History Project of Horry County*, Dr. Leroy Upperman, M.D., a Wilmington physician and surgeon and the last survivor of the Atlantic Beach Company, signed over the deed for restricted land that the town has since used for a playground on Thirty-first Avenue. On August 16, 1984, the town paid him $15,750 for Lot No. 61 of the Pearl Beach Section, which had been conveyed to him on April 3, 1953. It was only to be used for residential purposes, as a clubhouse (not a hotel), or a boarder's house. Luvenia Stanley is pictured 40 years ago in front of Tony's Motel. (Stanley.)

Halestine Tyson Cox (pictured age 10), great-niece of Mayor Cleveland "Jersey" Stevens, noted his work with U.S. Department of Agriculture, with legal services, as a public defender for 10 years, and with the Waccamaw Equal Opportunity Commission. He belonged to the Kappa Alpha Psi fraternity, South Carolina Bar, and National Trial Lawyers Association. He served four years in the navy and three in the air force. He had four daughters: Paula, Stefani, Valarie, and Natasha. (Halestine Tyson Cox.)

Marcus Graham (pictured age 10) holds up a bible and cash he received when he was baptised at First Missionary Baptist Church. Harvey Gantt, renowned architect, former mayor of Charlotte, and twice candidate for the U.S. Senate against the late Jesse Helms, came here. Elizabeth Leland, in *The Vanishing Coast*, quotes him regarding his "plan for an entertainment center . . . that would be a kind of museum. 'It will never be a totally black town anymore.' His parents Christopher and Wilhelmenia loaded their '51 Ford station wagon with him and his four sisters . . . and drove north from Charleston past a hundred miles of beach to the only stretch of South Carolina that welcomed blacks." The town rejected his Keenan Plan. (Stanley.)

Pictured is Deloris Castella Williams, a native Charlestonian and the sister of "Sam" Holmes. (Stanley.)

Pictured is Samuella Williams Holmes, a native Charlestonian on staff at the historic Jenkins Institute (home of the Jenkins Orphanage Band) and on the Charleston County Planning Commission. Jannie Isom said to ABHS, "Like I keep telling people, we didn't put that fence up. The fence was put up by North Myrtle Beach. We didn't have anything to do with that. I guess they were trying to keep us on one side and keep them on the other." Samuella might have seen the fence dividing Atlantic Beach from Crescent Beach where Holiday Inn (now Bay Watch) stands. No gates can come through to Windy Hill on the other side of Atlantic Beach. Councilman P. D. Mitchell's concerns about realtor Dick Hester were thus: "Money is not the issue. They want the whole waterfront. If they get it, they've got everything. We'd be pushed back across the highway," quoted the *Sarasota Herald Tribute*. (Stanley.)

Earl Gore (1928–2000), born in Columbus County, was the son of the late Peter and Carrie Gore. Earl married the late Gracie Riggins of Brooksville, Little River, South Carolina. Earl left two daughters, Bertha and Mary Ann. Earl worked hard and loved people and friends. He loved Atlantic Beach—"the only place he needs to be—dancing, sitting back, enjoying life and listening at the music." (Delois Jenerette Gore.)

Lloyd Gore (1927–2008), Earl's brother, was born in Brunswick County. He grew up on a farm and married Estermae Hill Gore, who bore him twins (Ardell and Ralph). Lloyd remarried to Edna Dupree from McClellanville, with whom he had five children—Christine, Jimmy, Joseph, Delois, and Ricky. There are many Gore (fondly called "Go") families with ties to Atlantic Beach. (Gore.)

Edna Dupree Gore (1932–2001) is with her son, Rodell Dupree (half-brother to Lloyd's five children). Waddie Harrison Gore (1887–1970), not pictured and not related to these Gores, purchased a lot from the Atlantic Beach Company in 1946. He went to school in Brunswick County and received his formal education from Fayetteville State University. He founded the First Missionary Baptist Church and moved to the beach to pursue his business interests (pavilion). Gore was a member of the Silver Star Masonic Lodge No. 333 and a Shriner. His two-story building still stands on Thirtieth Avenue and Front Street. (Gore.)

Lloyd, his wife, Edna, and her sister Louise pose in front of a house backdrop. Lloyd worked as a fisherman on a fish boat in Louisiana and returned to Southport, North Carolina, as a longshoreman, for which he received a certificate of appreciation. Lloyd's hobbies were playing the harmonica, fishing, picking the guitar, singing, dancing, and working. His favorite hangout was Atlantic Beach. (Gore.)

Lillian (in pedal-pushers) and George Myers are Delois's aunt and uncle. There are many Gore families to mention who are not shown and not related to this Gore family. Some with Atlantic Beach ties include Vander Moore Gore, former town councilman; his sister Hazel Gore and her son Lee Vander Bellamy Gore; Deloria Gore, who was married to Ranson Rowell Jr.; and property owner Daniel Vincent Gore, whose late father, Daniel, and Lee Grant Gore (unrelated to Daniel) were both petitioner signatories to the town charter. (Gore.)

Edna Dupree Gore, shown with her baby Christine, worked for Jim Lewis and Jeffroe Whitmore. She fried fish for the tourists, good fish sandwiches. Edna also had to load up drink machines. Christine Gore Hewitt (born 1954 in Brunswick County, North Carolina, owns and operates a child care center. Her children B. J. (Barbara Jane), Jody, and Kelly Hewett help her and sometimes her husband, Merrvis Hewett, too. (Gore.)

Janie Gore was married to Ardell Gore and was part of the family for years. (Gore.)

Delois Gore's "Auntie Weiz" in a white dress and heels is Louise Geralds. Raymond Gore (1935–2006), unrelated to these Gores, was the son of Bricey and Carrie Gore and was born in the Brooksville section of Horry County. He was predeceased by two brothers (Thelton, Pavilion) and Lishus, and four sisters. He had four sons, five daughters, and a wife, Linda. (Gore.)

Edward Gore (1940–2005), the baby boy of the late Peter and Carrie Gore, was known as "Buddy." He moved to Melbourne, Florida, where he worked hard as a contractor operating heavy machinery. Buddy was his own boss; he operated his own nightclub. Buddy loved music and cars. On holidays, when Buddy came home, he came to Atlantic Beach—"the place to be for fun and enjoyment," he would always say. (Gore.)

Johnnie Gore, the son of the late Peter and Carrie Gore, went to Mount Vernon, New York. He became a general contractor—moving people, landscaping, gardening, towing, and ceiling washing. He and his wife, Corine, were rewarded for helping others. Their hangout was Atlantic Beach. Johnnie's hobbies are dancing, singing, working, and having a blast on Atlantic Beach. One of Johnnie Gore's best hits was a song by Otis Redding: "I can't get no satisfaction, I tried, I tried, I tried." (Gore.)

Candy Marie Gore (left) is Marie's daughter, and Terry Wilson (right) is Juanita's daughter and the niece of Marie Gore, daughter of the late Peter and Carrie Gore (Delois's aunt). Eloise Gore (unrelated to these Gores) taught for 30 years in the Carolinas—mostly in Columbus County (North Carolina), but some in Horry County (South Carolina). (Gore.)

Marie Gore (born 1935) is the daughter of the late Peter and Carrie Gore. She is the mother of two, Candy Marie and Joyce Gore, and sports a big Afro and glasses. Marie always stayed around home to see after her mother and take care of her family. She was born and raised in Brunswick County. She also took pictures on Atlantic Beach and enjoyed being there. It was a pleasure, one of her best places to be. (Gore.)

Joyce Selena Gore (born 1954 in Brunswick County) looks like a ballerina in this Atlantic Beach souvenir picture. She is the daughter of Arrie G. Hill and Marie Gore. Joyce stayed in New Jersey for 30 years. She had two daughters: Elaine and Lachelle. (Gore.)

Delois Gore (right) and her brother Ricky Gore (left) are the children of Edna and Lloyd Gore. They were born in Brunswick County in 1958 and 1959, respectively. Delois worked many years at the Myrtle Beach Hilton in housekeeping. She is studying medical billing and medical transcriptionist work. She has two sons, Montel McAtee and Jay Jenerette. Ricky is married to Barbara Ann Gore, and they have three children—daughters Casaundre and LeeAnn and son Terrell. Ricky does light carpet and landscaping work. (Gore.)

Joseph Gore (born 1957) was the son of the late Lloyd and Edna Gore and brother to Delois and Ricky. He has two sons, Jimmy and Joseph. He is a carpet and tile installer. Mayor Emery Gore (unrelated) belonged to Silver Star Lodge No. 333, Prince Hall, and Long Bay Hunting Club. He was a Mason, a trustee and Building Committee member of St. Paul AME Church, and he served in World War II. (Gore.)

Here are siblings Jimmy Gore, who with wife Marilyn ran Studio 44 nightclub, and Christine Gore Hewett. (Gore.)

Ardell Gore (born 1949), son of the late Lloyd Gore and his first wife, Estermae, is a twin to Ralph. He has his own business called Gore's Repair. His business consists of painting, plumbing, hauling, all house improvements, power wash, carpentry, landscaping, and backhoe and dozer work. Albert L. "Cat" Gore (unrelated, pictured on page 73) and Lee Vander (Gore) Bellamy tell great stories of Lee "coming out of his diapers on the beach" and flying into a hurricane wind like Superman with friends Cat and James Sinclair—bodies straight out, lifted off the ground, totally unafraid. (Gore.)

Juanita Gore Wilson (1936–2001), the daughter of the late Peter and Carrie Gore, was born in Brunswick County. She had one daughter, Terry, with whom she lived in Miami. She loved music, dancing, and talking to people. She loved dogs and just enjoyed life. She traveled back and forth to see her family and especially loved coming to Atlantic Beach, where she took many pictures. (Gore.)

Edna Gore was the mother of Christine, Jimmy, Joseph, Delois, and Ricky. Unrelated to these Gores, E&E owner Eloise Gore (1926?–2006) was born in Latta and married the late mayor Emery Gore. She received her degrees in North Carolina—bachelor's from Livingstone College, Salisbury, and master's from the Agricultural and Technical (A&T) University, Greensboro. She was treasurer of Moonlight Chapter No. 168 Order of Eastern Star, Prince Hall Affiliation. She belonged to the AME Church, St. Paul and then Weston Chapel. (Gore.)

Lloyd Gore was the father of Christine, Jimmy, Joseph, Delois, and Ricky. Emery Gore (1923–2000), not related, was born to Charley Gore and Lila Stanley Gore, the third of 10 children. He built E&E for his wife of 47 years, Eloise, as a honeymoon present. He was sworn in as the first elected mayor of Atlantic Beach and later served as a member of the Zoning Committee and as the building inspector. (Gore.)

Peter Gore (1895–1982), son of the late Jackson and Fannie Gore, was born in Brunswick County, North Carolina. His marriage to Carrie Frink yielded nine children, including Lloyd, Marie, Peter, Johnnie, Earl, and Edward. Peter worked hard to take care of this family. Carrie loved cooking for her family and always loved a garden of green vegetables. Peter's favorite place and fun time was Atlantic Beach. (Gore.)

Current mayor Retha Pierce (left) watches as Rev. Windy Price (right) officiates at a 2006 memorial program at the Chick-fil-A in North Myrtle Beach where Carma Yvette Russell, a slain victim of domestic violence, had been employed. Price also held a 2004 memorial service for victim Juice Nallo at her Atlantic Beach Christian Methodist Episcopal (CME) Church on Thirtieth Avenue. Price placed her church right in the middle of town to help the needy. She still provides a strong voice and presence, along with her husband, Darnell, and children Victoria, Darnell Jr. ("Man Man") and son Zephaniah ("Zep"). (ABHS.)

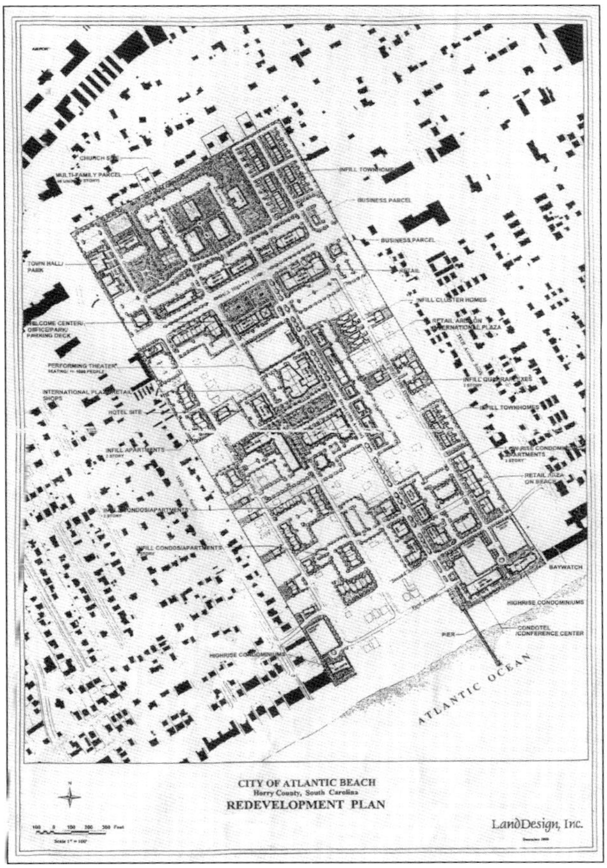

"When Jim Crow was banished, black tourists found more (elsewhere) and the Black Pearl went into decline," reports Will Moredock in *Banana Republic*. There are 400 parcels in the 96-acre town, with approximately 168 owners, unlike one with Burroughs and Chapin's Myrtle Beach. "Master Plan" and "moratorium" had become watchwords to answer questions about how to develop—Who? When? With what or whose money? Waccamaw Regional Council of Government has been part of the process. (Stanley.)

Atlantic Beach remained a source of entertainment for African Americans even after integration. This parade features real Milwaukee Clydesdale horses. (Stanley.)

Atlantic Beach also remained a source of cultural and heritage pride with this marching band. In the left background is part of the two-story Rowell Grocery, and to its right is a towering Ferris wheel that used to be one of the main attractions. (Rowell.)

Three

INTEGRATION
THE TOWN AND REVITALIZATION EFFORTS

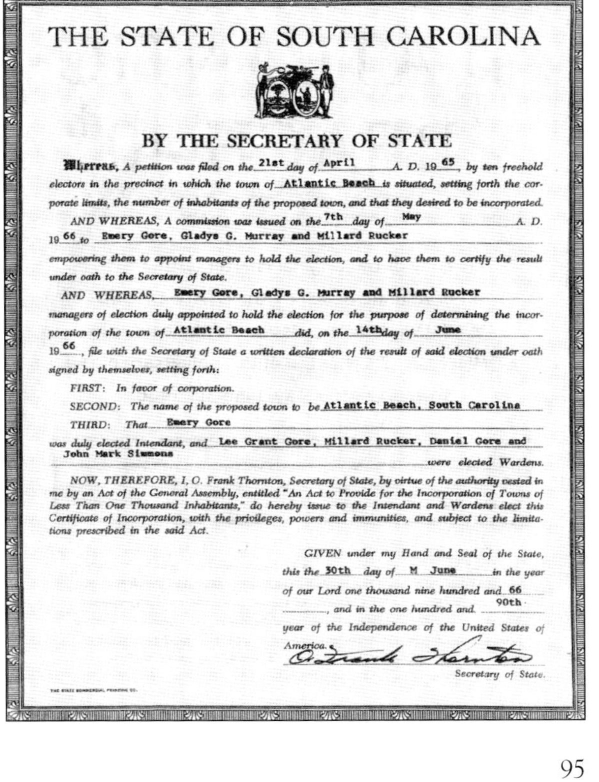

THE STATE OF SOUTH CAROLINA

BY THE SECRETARY OF STATE

Whereas, A petition was filed on the 21st day of April A. D. 1965, by ten freehold electors in the precinct in which the town of Atlantic Beach is situated, setting forth the corporate limits, the number of inhabitants of the proposed town, and that they desired to be incorporated.

AND WHEREAS, A commission was issued on the 7th day of May A. D. 1966 to Emery Gore, Gladys G. Murray and Millard Rucker empowering them to appoint managers to hold the election, and to have them to certify the result under oath to the Secretary of State.

AND WHEREAS, Emery Gore, Gladys G. Murray and Millard Rucker managers of election duly appointed to hold the election for the purpose of determining the incorporation of the town of Atlantic Beach did, on the 14th day of June 1966, file with the Secretary of State a written declaration of the result of said election under oath signed by themselves, setting forth:

FIRST: In favor of corporation.

SECOND: The name of the proposed town to be Atlantic Beach, South Carolina

THIRD: That Emery Gore was duly elected Intendant, and Lee Grant Gore, Millard Rucker, Daniel Gore and John Mark Simmons were elected Wardens.

NOW, THEREFORE, I, O. Frank Thornton, Secretary of State, by virtue of the authority vested in me by an Act of the General Assembly, entitled "An Act to Provide for the Incorporation of Towns of Less Than One Thousand Inhabitants," do hereby issue to the Intendant and Wardens elect this Certificate of Incorporation, with the privileges, powers and immunities, and subject to the limitations prescribed in the said Act.

GIVEN under my Hand and Seal of the State, this the 30th day of M June in the year of our Lord one thousand nine hundred and 66, and in the one hundred and 90th year of the Independence of the United States of America.

O. Frank Thornton
Secretary of State.

THE STATE COMMERCIAL PRINTING CO.

The Town of Atlantic Beach incorporated on June 30, 1966. For 30 years, Atlantic Beach had no town government—elected officials, mayor, or town council—no property taxes, no police or fire department, and no building inspectors, yet it managed, survived, and thrived. So why incorporate? Was it to protect against takeover, to apply for government grants, to police increasing crime rates to get better insurance rates, or for prestige? (South Carolina Secretary of State.)

Franklin Roosevelt DeWitt (1936–2008) guided the charter process. He was born in Horry County, the 12th of 15 children of the late Matthew A. and Rebecca Hughes DeWitt. A graduate of Whittemore High School, DeWitt served in the U.S. Air Force. He received his bachelor's degree in 1962 and doctor of law degree in 1964 from South Carolina State College. Franklin was a trial attorney under Attorney General Robert "Bobby" Kennedy before becoming town attorney. (Willa DeWitt.)

DeWitt was actively involved in all the bar associations, Kappa Alpha Psi Fraternity, the NAACP, and the SCSU Alumni Association. Pictured is W. P. Johnson, father of Willa Johnson DeWitt, Ph.D. in education and a retired assistant superintendent of schools. Willa was married 47 years to Franklin DeWitt and assisted him with the town incorporation process. They have two daughters, Rosalyn and Sharolyn. (Johnson.)

Ground-breaking of the town hall in 1971 was attended by the following, from left to right: (first row) unidentified, Phyonica Montgomery, Lefuel Sketers, Willie Bellamy, Willie Stevens, Joe Montgomery, Franklin DeWitt, Rev. Luther Small, Jeffro Hart, Mary Glass, John Mark Simmons; (second row) James Bradley, unidentified, Ethel Lucas Woods, two unidentified, Thaxton Dixon, JoAnn Williams, unidentified, Mable Watson, unidentified, Jim Lewis, unidentified, and Millard Rucker. (Stanley.)

Strom Thurmond, on the far right, was instrumental in getting federal funds to help build the community center in 1977. The town received three grants, respectively, for drainage, streets, and economic development: $436,577 in 1998, $500,000 in 1997, and $250,000 in 1998 from Horry County Community Development Block Grant (CDBG). (Earlene Woods.)

Carrine Rucker (1930–2006, at right), born in Wampee, received her bachelor of arts degree in elementary education from Allen University in Columbia. She belonged to Atlantic Beach First Baptist Church. She and her husband, Millard, had one son, Millard Rucker Jr. of Charleston, and four daughters: Patrilla (Brutus) Judd; Rosa (Bernard) Rucker Lightfoot, Ph.D.; Ruth (Freddie) Wilson; and Fay O'Dell (deceased 2008). (ABHS.)

Councilman Mark Simmons (1921–2001) is with "special friend" Rosa Stanley. Simmons was the son of the late Annie Bell Spivey Simmons and George Scott Simmons. He attended the Myrtle Beach Colored School and graduated from Barber Scotia College in North Carolina. Simmons was a World War II veteran and worked in several businesses and golf clubs. He belonged first to Mount Olive AME Church and later St. Paul AME Church. (Stanley.)

Mayor Joe Elliott Montgomery (born 1942) served four terms from 1976 to 1995. He is an Allen University graduate in social studies. He and his wife, Phyonica Toatley, have one son, Charles J. Montgomery. Montgomery was a teacher in the Horry County School District and a member of the Kappa Alpha Psi Fraternity. He still lives in Atlantic Beach, with frequent visits back home to Hemingway, South Carolina. (Stanley.)

Mayor Joe Montgomery is with an unidentified guest speaker believed to be an actor from television's *Miami Vice*. In his first term, he worked with Atlantic Beach Development Corporation and its president, Leslie H. McIver; with the Atlantic Beach Entrepreneurial Development Corporation, which is made up of council members; and with David Richardson, realtor. Montgomery is most known for promoting the Keenan Plan, formulated by black architect Harvey Gantt and defeated by the council because of the community fear of eminent domain. (Stanley.)

Junior Grissett was a police officer. Contracting out police to North Myrtle Beach or Horry County has been a continual controversy. Drugs and prostitution are the biggest crimes—"just like any other community," officials say. (Stanley.)

On the left, Councilman Lefuel Sketers (1907–1991) receives congratulations from Mayor Cleveland Stevens (1927–1991), whose term was from 1981 to 1985. Born in Loris, Stevens attended schools there and graduated from Williston High School in Wilmington, North Carolina. He received his undergraduate degree and law degree from South Carolina State College in Orangeburg. Lefuel Sketers (1907–1991) was the son of Mack and Cherry Frierson. He was married to Leah Mildred Lucas, and they had eight children—Eugene, Albert, John, Russell, James, Raymond, Joseph, and Dora Jacklyn Parker. He was a deacon at the First Missionary Baptist Church and served on town council for 11 years. (Skeeters.)

Luvenia Simmons, age eight, stands by an Atlantic Beach police car. Hotel Theresa, built in the 1940s, was the location of the first city hall, at Thirtieth and Ocean Avenues. Meetings were held downstairs; sleeping rooms were upstairs, Emma Lee Vereen informs. (Stanley.)

An excerpt of a Pat Robinson (pictured) poem reads: "Cleveland Stevens' was a great believer in the fact that even thru adversity, Atlantic Beach would make it. . . . When I think of a man, I think of Cleveland Stevens. . . . He reached to stranger(s) and befriended them, to show them no matter who he was they were somebody too. He reached to me a drug addict and. . . . I'm changed today I'm sober today, I'm a published writer today because Cleveland Stevens was one of those angels that God kept on sending to reach me in hopes Id see." (ABHS.)

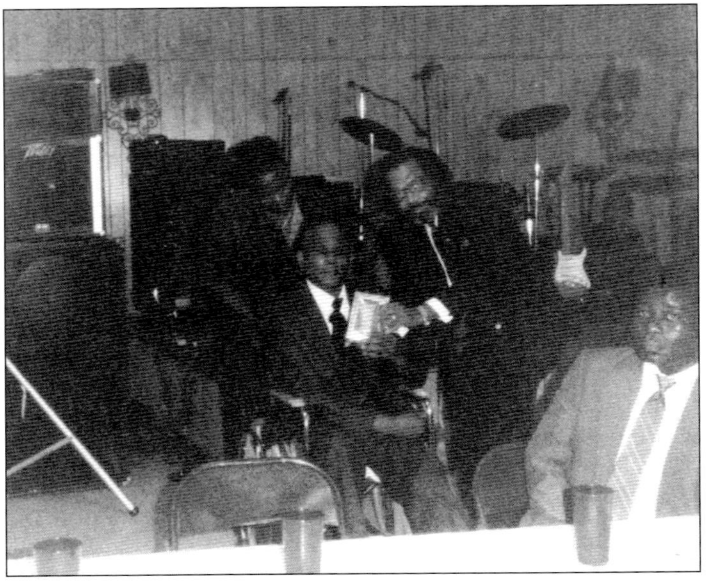

Councilman Jim Lewis (seated left, in wheelchair) is congratulated by his son Lenwood (standing on the left), and Rev. H. H. Singleton (standing in the center), NAACP president, for receiving a certificate of appreciation for service. Mayor Montgomery is seated on the right, in front. The first full-term mayor, Millard Rucker (1911–1996), the son of the late Rev. Robert Benjamin and Mary Louise Watson Rucker, chaired the Housing Authority and Waccamaw Planning Council. (Stanley.)

Councilman Mark Simmons holds his plaque with Councilman Jim Lewis and Lewis's son James Lenwood Lewis at the Atlantic Beach Community Center. Another councilman (not pictured) was Philbert D. Mitchell (1910–1987). "P. D" was the son of the late Martin Mitchell. He was educated in Robeson County and at Fayetteville Normal School. In 1939, he got a certificate from the Civilian Conservation Corps and married Violet Head. He was very active with First Missionary Baptist Church and served on council 12 years, 1967–1979. (Stanley.)

Punk's Patio was hit hard by Hurricane Hugo in 1989. The last wall of the patio filled with colorful graffiti and gutter language was torn down by town edict in 2002, and the perfectly fine wooden dance floor was trashed, explained Punk's nephew Reggie Dyson, because no one knew that anyone (like the new historical society) would have wanted to re-create Patio dancing. (Stanley.)

Punk's Patio lost a wall to Hurricane Hugo. Tony's Motel was soaked by Hurricane Hugo. Much of the development efforts in Atlantic Beach continue to be targets of bank "redlining"—withholding loan funds or insurance from neighborhood considered poor economic risks. In the last two pages of her *Myrtle Beach Greetings*, where Atlantic Beach is featured, Barbara F. Stokes quotes Earlene Woods: "The hurricane took the businesses, but integration took the people." (Stanley.)

Merlin Bellamy (born 1927) is synonymous with North Myrtle Beach, his birthplace. In 1950, Bellamy became the chief of police, the garbage truck driver, fire chief, and city promoter. His quick, decisive action during 1954's Hurricane Hazel earned him national acclaim. He started what is now the Can-Am Days (for Canadians), and the Harley-Davidson Rally (for motorcycle riders), writes R. Walter Hill. Shown is Merlin, his wife, Joyce, and their first great-grandchild, Jasmine, in 2006. (ABHS.)

George Latimer Jr. and his 5-year-old son Nigel are pictured at their well-kept family home on First Avenue, which has weathered many storms. George's grandparents, H. C. and Lillie Latimer, were 1930s purchasers of lots from George W. Tyson. With his mother, Edna, and brother Marvin, George runs the Latimer Funeral Home in Conway left them by George Sr. His daughter Bradleigh, age seven, is not shown. (ABHS.)

Involved since the 1970s, David Richardson became president of the Atlantic Beach Community Development Corporation (CDC) in 1994. *The Sun News* reported, "In 1999, he announced that advertisements would appear seeking tenants for a $2 million, 18,000 square foot building near town hall. Another proposed business, Sylvia's Restaurant based in New York, might come, too. . . . The CDC received . . . $250,000 from HUD . . . of a total of $750,000 since its inception." (Charleston Chronicle.)

John Sketers, elected to town council in 1976, voted in 1983 to enact a three-story height restriction on the oceanfront. Dick Hester planned a high-rise condominium-motel resort. Twice he was met with ongoing town ambivalence about "looking like Myrtle Beach." In 2001, Sketers voted to enact unlimited height. Then the town manager planned high-rise units on oceanfront land. Sketers later worked with realtor Joe Garrell on the Black Pearl development project, which did not come to fruition. (Charleston Chronicle.)

The 1950s E&E Motel's knotty pine wood interior, the Safari Room, is the brainchild of Elizabeth Williams Simpson, a self-taught interior designer who has transformed other rooms to individualized motifs. Her husband, Robert Simpson, is a self-taught mason, tile installer, and carpenter who moved from accounting into real estate. One famous E&E guest was Richard Burnside, whose work is part of 5,000 "outsider art" paintings hanging in all of the House of Blues establishments. Many of the rooms now have televisions, iceboxes, and microwaves. (Robert Simpson.)

The Simpsons also operate refurbished Express Inn in Gastonia, on I-85, some 20 minutes outside of Charlotte. They drove from Florida in search of the black beach they had heard about, but in 2005 Atlantic Beach oceanfront and Front Street property turned over to white developer owners. The Simpsons are active with NABHOOD, the National Association of Black Hotel Owners, Operators, and Developers. (Simpson.)

In front of her E&E motel sign stands Eloise Bethea Gore (right), with author Sherry Suttles (left). Gore wanted Ocean Boulevard opened, as did Katie Powell (1913–2003), born in Windsor, North Carolina, a retired schoolteacher and speech therapist with a bachelor's degree from Elizabeth City and a master's degree from New York University. Powell said, on opening Ocean Boulevard, "I'll be glad when they can go through (Windy Hill). Want to go to stores and things without having to go to 17 to Food Lion." (ABHS.)

Violet Head Mitchell (1919–2008), daughter of the late Robert C. and Marie D. Head, was born in Spartanburg. She married P. D. Mitchell in 1939 and moved to High Point, North Carolina. In 1970, they established the Parkview Motel (for sale) and Restaurant, on Thirty-first Avenue South, and Mitchell's Beverage Mart and Package Store on Highway 17. From left to right are Ms. Mitchell, her godson "Baker," and tenant Larry Smalls. Arthur Carr (not pictured) also visited with her often. (ABHS.)

In 2005, Amy Breunig purchased the Levon Motel at 603 Thirtieth Avenue (Front Street) from Pavilack Realty, with the influx of white developers, including Marathon Development, LaCasa, and then-partner David O'Connell. She also bought on Thirtieth: 401—Brown's Inn, Calep Brown; 405 and 407—Reverend Duren; 409—Atlantic Inn, realtor Mary Amos; and 507—The Manhattan, or Love's Nest, chiropractor Sam Arnold and Daisy Arnold (grandson). (Amy Breunig.)

Betty "Toby" (Rowell) Dixon serves Larry Smalls (left) and LaRue Sherman (right). On May 22, 2003—two years earlier to the day after the historical marker was erected at their suggestion—the state archives declared not a single building in Atlantic Beach would meet National Register designation requirements. The Rowell family has renovated this restaurant adjacent to Hotel Marshall and the Off the Hook bar on the corner of Thirtieth Avenue and Second Street. Dixon's daughter Octavia, "Cricket," helps out like Atlantic Beach kids do. (ABHS.)

Owner Amy Breunig worked two years to unveil the true Levon exterior—brick. Plantings adorn the entrance as in the heyday. Though a trained nurse, she has been an avid real estate developer and property manager. She and her mother, Bridgette Breunig, have made a major turnaround in the crime problems as well. Breunig has a bachelor of science degree from Sacred Heart University, Fairfield, Connecticut. (Breunig.)

Brenda Rowell-Bromell, the Marshall owner, was born to Ranson and Bernice Rowell and raised in Marion with sister Toby and brothers Jerry and Ranson Jr. She told ABHS interviewer Veronica Gerald, "A man who used to work for Miller [Beer Company] named Mr. Wilhart told my father, 'you run a business so good, you need to go to the beach. It's a black beach. You could make some money down there'." (ABHS.)

This October Fish Fry, still a favorite in Atlantic Beach, was held for the November 2003 election campaign. The race for council and mayor seats was contested all the way to the Supreme Court (as it was in 2007). Pictured on the far right, in a wheelchair, is the secretary of the historical society, Housing Authority resident Tema Lewis Hill. (ABHS.)

The Mayo High School 52nd reunion was held, in part, at Atlantic Beach to recall "the good times there," said Mary L. Warsaw-Capers. Town hall referred the group to the historical society for a tour and organized a special "October Fish Fry" on November 18, 2006, including traditional patio dancing on the oceanfront. Atlantic Beach Company's Dr. Robert K. Gordon smiled down to see his fellow Mayo alums so well treated. (ABHS.)

Emily Morse Stanley (center) and Denise Stanley attend the fish fry in the courtyard of the Skeeters' Motel and Lounge. Housing Authority residents are sometimes a pivotal voting bloc. Emily's Sean, Tanisha, and Mariah Bryant, and Shaquita and Derrick Stanley (an ordained minister at 18) are active with the CME church. (ABHS.)

The premier chef for an Atlantic Beach fish fry is Thelton "Foxx" Gore, one of 11 sons whose dad, Melton, ran a pavilion back in the day. He is shown here at the 2006 Mayo reunion on the left preparing another batch with town police officers Michele Coleman and Charles Bryant. Foxx works with Horry County. Other good fish fry chefs are Pat "Lil Bit" (6'), Miss Fannie, Brenda Rowell-Bromell, and Retha Pierce, who also makes the best Retha's Delight cake in the world. (ABHS.)

For more than 60 years, the Atlantic Beach First Missionary Baptist Church has served. Three recently deceased members are (at left) Rev. Richard Bessant, (behind him) trustee Ronald Isom (former police chief and town historian), and (at right) Ora Hooker (1932–2006). Hooker was a member of the Eastern Star (New Hope Chapter OES, No. 79) and Housing Authority commissioner. Pastor Smart Smalls (center) speaks with James Drumgoole, a 30-year property owner. (Floyd.)

Nicole Kenion and her son Chris are Housing Authority residents from Detroit. Nicole studies nursing. Chris is in the Job Corps. Of the original 52 units built in 1984, a total of 14 units were closed down in 2008 on the east side of Highway 17 to be sold. Housing Authority residents have been a major voting bloc that will be lost with its closing. (ABHS.)

"Li'l Bit" Patricia Edwards and "Miss Fannie" Smith are great fish fry chefs. They are shown here at the November 2003 council candidate's political rally.

Hubert Williams Jr. (rear center) traveled from Columbia to preside over meetings of the Atlantic Beach Property Owners Association. Supreme Court chief justice Ernest Finney was president of the Atlantic Beach Landowners Association, in which Ronald Taylor (of Columbia) and Harriett Cochrane (of Charleston) were active. Ninety percent of the landowners are absentees. Hubert Williams Sr. was one of the first 1940s purchasers from the Atlantic Beach Company. (ABHS.)

Pictured from left to right are Shaquita Stanley, Dora Gore, and Ashley Gore. Nearby Atlantic Water Sports draws mostly white tourists 100 to 300 feet over the ocean parasailing. Owner Jeff Ray dropped out of school to start this business and now has a crew of 20, who operate speedboats, rent umbrellas, and serve as lifeguards throughout North Myrtle Beach. He pays substantial annual town business license fees. (ABHS.)

Janie Macon, caterer and former Housing Authority resident, leads the first ever SunFun Atlantic Beach girls' drill team at the head of the Celebrate U.S. float. Janie started the group because she was in one started by Ms. Grantham. Macon's two young daughters, "Lulu" and Kayla, watched on the sidelines. Atlantic Beach and Myrtle Beach are closing down public housing (North Myrtle Beach never had it). (ABHS.)

These boys were persuaded to attend the 2004 SunFun Celebrate Unity event on the Grand Strand in Chapin Park, Myrtle Beach, sponsored by the Atlantic Beach Historical Society. Their big question about the Scots-Irish bagpiper performers was, "Why do they wear skirts?" Former mayor pro tem Jake Evans has coached many basketball teams in the North Myrtle Beach League, winning championships three years in a row. (ABHS.)

Marie Sadler (second row, far left), at SunFun, is the cofounder with her husband, "Pop" Sadler, of the Greenville Community Combined Youth Organization. This well-regarded Charlotte couple led their famed marching band through Atlantic Beach streets (heyday style) many times. The Sadlers recount hilarious stories to their children and grandchildren about the times their parents had at the beach. Marie Sadler started the Atlantic Beach Historical Society. (ABHS.)

Dora Roncancio and Ana Moore, realtor, were the belles of the ball on all of the Celebrate Unity floats at SunFun and in the Preserving Memories program in 2007. They are Spanish-speaking transplants from Colombia who perform traditional, rural, classic dances each year. They are very active in the Trinity Catholic Church. Atlantic Beach has a large Spanish-bilingual population. (ABHS.)

Bobbi Bernstein and Jerry Edwards perform together at the 2004 Celebrate US SunFun event. They are both followers of Meher Baba at the Spiritual Center in North Myrtle Beach. Their fusion music of jazz, folk, blues, and spiritual songs exemplify the mix of people and culture that some hope to bring to a 21st-century Black Pearl. (ABHS.)

Carolina Knight Riders president Mack Vereen, the Popular Sportsman nightclub owner on the left, with John Glover (right), led the first ever motorcycle riders in the 2003 Myrtle Beach SunFun Festival. The ABHS Celebrate Unity on the Strand entry was the first ever multicultural float and included Waccamaw Indians chief Buster Hatcher. The Sportsman held a second annual Fall Dance in Atlantic Beach in 2008. (ABHS.)

From left to right, now mayor Retha Pierce, hotel owner Thaxton Dixon, and then-councilwoman Sherry A. Suttles enjoy Bikefest 2007. Dixon painted his red-brick Riviera Motel grey. His fishing partner, Frances ("Mal") Parker, joins him on the beach. Ninety-year-old Thaxton Dixon also likes to fish with his nephew Harris ("J") when he comes down from Greensboro to help manage the motel during the BikeFest "full house." (Stanley.)

Latonia Peterson (left) presides over a meeting of the Atlantic Beach Historical Society at Ryan's Restaurant. She moved to Myrtle Beach from Chicago and sought a role to play with the preservation of the historically black town. Her greatest legacy was the installation of the South Carolina Historical Marker. Paul Curry, resident gadfly of the community on the right, makes many valuable volunteer contributions. (ABHS.)

Horry County Museum hosted a first ever, three-month photography display in 2003, sponsored by the Atlantic Beach Historical Society, which featured photographs from AfroFest 1993 and excerpts from the ABHS Oral History Elders Project. From left to right are state senator Richard "Dick" Elliott; Sherry Suttles; Stuart Pabst, museum director; an unidentified museum representative; Mayor Irene Armstrong; Gloria Lance, AfroFest and councilmember; Beverly Clark; and Alice Graham, AfroFest. (ABHS.)

Jowanda Jackson (left) was one of the first active supporters of the historical society, permitting her twin daughters, Parris and Porscha, to go on field trips. She moved to the Housing Authority from Michigan and works at Food Lion. They moved out of town with the closing of the Eastside units. "Ms. Kat" Hairston had held the community center post, with then–police chief husband—now in Eastover—so the historical society filled a void. (ABHS.)

The Beach Music Association International presented its first ever check, in 2006 for $4,000, to the Atlantic Beach Historical Society to "keep on doing what you are doing." Pictured from left to right are Hilda Carter, columnist; unidentified; Harry Turner, historical society president; Sherry Suttles, historian; Billy Scott, board chairman; and unidentified. (ABHS.)

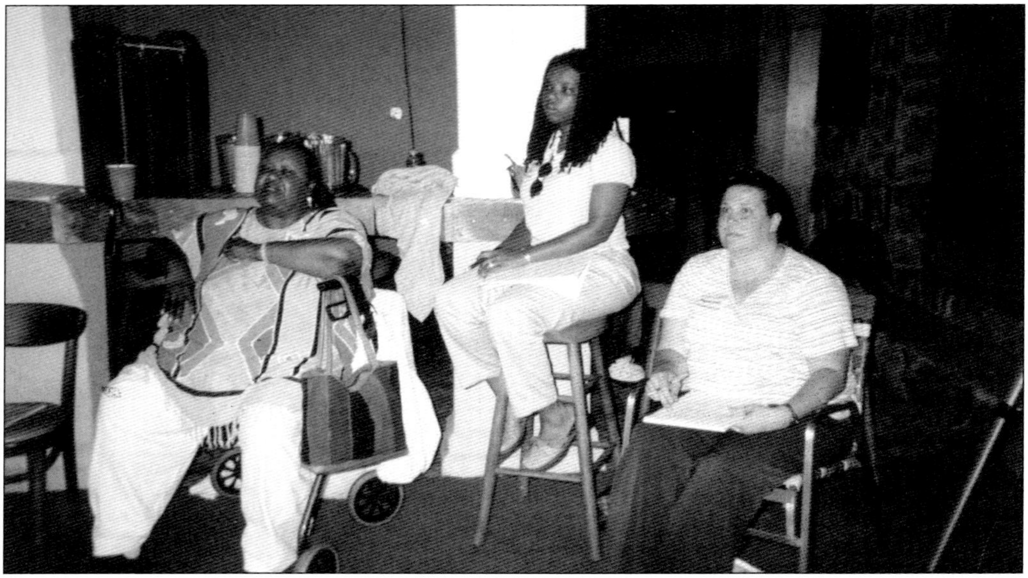

Preserving Memories was the first time the historical society began to collect memorabilia before the proposed building demolition. "Celebrate US" continued at Kingston Plantation (SunFun was cancelled), Listening to Marsha, and Michael Phelts, from sister city American Beach, Florida, are, from left to right, Vermelle "Bunny" Rodrigues, the Gullah/Geechee Festival coordinator; and two state archives staffers, Leah Brown and Rebekah Dobrasko, at Brenda's Kitchen. (ABHS.)

On May 22, 2005, the Atlantic Beach Historical Society proudly erected the first Grand Strand Historical Marker approved by the South Carolina Department of Archives and History. Sherry Suttles researched and wrote the history and raised funds—from Conway National Bank, Sam's Club, and David A. Graham III (Suttles's nephew). It is located in front of town hall on Thirtieth Avenue at Highway 17. "Pop" Sadler is second from left, in the far right rear. From left to right are Jake Evans, then-mayor pro tem; Marie Sadler, ABHS co-chair; Marilyn Hatley, North Myrtle Beach mayor; and Irene Evans Armstrong, then three-term mayor. (ABHS.)

Dorothy Floyd, historical society treasurer, in Dr. Jesse Williams's home, hosts Preserving Memories. Williams and Dr. Noralean Williams rebuilt Sam Thaggard's oceanfront home. Next door, Poterresia McNeill and, on Thirty-second, Nick Davis built the first new homes in the 1990s. In 2004, Councilman Donnell Thompson, retired Indianapolis Colts football Hall of Famer and his administrator wife, Carr, built a new house on Thirty-first Avenue; and Fayetteville military retiree Vernon Fisher, with his pharmacist wife, is building one of the new huge mansions on Thirty-second Avenue. Some upfitting has been done at the Beck home on First Avenue facing the Ocean. "Humanitarian, physician, political power broker" were words used to describe Dr. Roswell Nathaniel Beck Sr. at his funeral on January 17, 2003. A spokeswoman for U.S. Congressman James Clyburn's office added, "I can also remember when politicians running for office attended stump meetings at his beach house in Atlantic Beach." (ABHS.)

Seated from left to right are Brian Shaw from the Atlantic Beach Chamber of Commerce; author Sherry Suttles; and Yolanda Guyton of the U.S. Postal Service in Windy Hill. Adult entertainment—Crazy Horse and Excitement Video—is the financial mainstay of Atlantic Beach. Blacks sold prime land years ago, and on Highway 17, to Tebele Enterprises (Sand Beach Wear, China Dragon, Thee Pawn Shop, Blockbuster) and Pavilack Realty. (ABHS.)

Norman Pearsall (1957–2008), known as "Tree" for his 6-foot, 7-inch height (on the far left), rarely smiled but was the life of the party, dancing and talking in intelligent "gibberish." Tree, a first cousin of Michael Jordan and skilled handyman, was homeless. He and Jamie ("Mimi") Wilson (second from left) attend a "For Old Times' Sake" dance, which ended after 20 years, by founders Jane and John Sketers, later named official town historian by the town council. (ABHS.)

Leo McFadden teaches Sherry Suttles "poker" at the historical society Holiday Game Party in Black Magic Disco. His sister-in-law, Pat Mallett, is a social studies teacher at North Myrtle Beach High School. Deborah Serra opened Mr. G's Ice Cream across the highway when another town moratorium blocked her. Long-timer Chuck Freeman, Allstate, and the oceanfront developers were set back, too. (ABHS.)

Jannie Isom (born 1943), a school bus driver and midday worker, was born in Clarendon County. She said in an ABHS interview, "It could be better if all of us would get together and do whatever we need to do. . . . You have to be together as one to make things move. Some of the local government—the council members—are not together. If they're not together, we're not together." (Museum.)

Willie Isom (1942–2004), a retired photograph technician for the government, was born in Onslow County, North Carolina. He and his wife, Jannie, raised two sons and two daughters: a police firefighter, a real estate agent, an assistant manager at CVS drugstore, and one in the U.S. Air Force. (Museum.)

Russell Skeeters (some families spell it Sketers) was born in 1940 in Florence and, with his wife, Elenora, from McComb, Mississippi, raised four children: Richard, Pamela, Melissa, and Keldrick. He said, "Well, Atlantic Beach is a beautiful place to be. I want to be here to the end. I love it, and eventually, I hope something's going to happen down here. I would hope that our elected officials let the people know what's going on before they make decisions that would be harmful to the community." "We had Maurice and the Zodiacs, Bo Didley, James Brown, Hank Ballard and the Midnighters," Skeeters told ABHS. The Skeeters family holdings, since 1951, recently sold after 10 years of heir's property legal battles, a typical problem with preserving African American–owned land. Skeeters, trustee, is cooking fish at the First Missionary Baptist Church. (Stanley.)

Pictured is MaVynee Betsch (1934–2005), who succeeded in efforts to "Save American Beach." On Amelia Island in Fernandina Beach, Florida, this "sister city" was founded about the same time as Atlantic Beach (1930s), same 96 acres, 400 parcels, and 200 owners. Betsch, "The Beach Lady," literally slept on the sand to keep developers away and get designation through the A. L. Lewis Historical Society. (ABHS.)

Maurice Williams (pictured) of The Zodiacs, performing since 50 years ago, is most famous for "Stay." He only ever racked up one major national hit on the pop charts. That song, "Stay," became one of the classic singles in the history of rock—a number one hit upon its release in 1960. Etrulia Dozier (born 1930) told the ABHS basically that black people should "stay": "I hope that the people who are still at Atlantic Beach focus in on the heritage and legacy of a small, but interesting and a very precious piece of the history of black folks who have lived in this area, who have owned property. I'm going to write in big letters to my children, 'Do not sell this property unless they give you $100,000,000 and you can go next door and buy something'." (Scott.)

George W. Tyson and Roxie Ballen Tyson are saints. No one knows when or how Atlantic Beach became "The Black Pearl," a nickname meaning exclusivity, but the Tahitian description for a "black pearl" is that it includes every color in the rainbow. Perhaps Atlantic Beach will stay predominantly black owned but diversified to meet the times. (ABHS.)

ABOUT THE ORGANIZATION

The Atlantic Beach Historical Society, Inc., and Atlantic Beach Chamber of Commerce were created at the same time by Sherry A. Suttles after she was recruited to apply for the town manager job in 2000.

Instead Suttles became enamored with the colorful history of the town. Through Brenda Rowell-Bromell, owner of Hotel Marshall, Suttles first worked with Jim Goodman on REHAB (Restore Historic Atlantic Beach). Its auxiliary, ABHS, became incorporated in 2001 and received IRS 501 c3 tax-exempt status in 2002. The mission statement is: "To preserve the history of the Coastal Carolinas African American Heritage through oral histories and memorabilia, year-round family events, and personal and real property."

The historical society has accomplished most of its goals, as a separate entity from town government, it should be noted. In 2004, grants came from South Carolina Humanities for oral histories, from S.C. Arts and City of Myrtle Beach for SunFun Parade and Celebrate Unity on the Strand in Chapin Park.

ABHS began taking care of the children when town hall cut back programming—Freewood Farms, ice cream, and Myrtle Beach Christian Retreat during BikeFest. Their first book was a historical coloring book called *Turtle vs. Bike Power* (Afterward, a coloring book by Horry County Conway National Bank was found with no AB reference.)

In 2003, ABHS coordinated the first ever Atlantic Beach photographical exhibit at the Horry County Museum in Conway, South Carolina. The AfroFest 1993 Committee coordinator, Alice Graham, donated the pictures, and the ABHS oral history interview excerpts were a hit.

By far, the greatest triumph of the historical society was getting a marker erected on May 22, 2005, in front of town hall, the first ever on the Grand Strand. Suttles raised the $1600, $500 each, from Sam's, Conway National Bank, and her nephew David Alexander Graham III from Detroit, Michigan. Nearly 100 attendees participated in the ceremony.

Other accomplishments included a children's play on March 4, 2006, regrettably marred by the shooting at the CME church of Carma Russell. Fortunately, ABHS raised $10,000 anonymously to help their children in Alabama. In 2006, Billy Scott and Harry Turner, of Beach Music Association International, gave $4,000 to the historical society.

In 2007, Rebekah Dobrasko of the South Carolina Department of Archives and History (SCDAH) referred the town of Atlantic Beach to ABHS for input into the proposed demolition of several properties. This was the first time that artifacts could be officially identified and removed for archival purposes, as shown therein from Esau Jenkins's motel. On June 1, 2007, ABHS hosted a "Preserving Memories" event at Hotel Marshall that featured Rebekah and Leah Brown, African American coordinator for SCDAH. Special guests included Michael and Marsha Phelts of American Beach, Florida. Some stayed over for the International Dance Exhibit that succeeded the cancelled SunFun parade. A colorful brochure was designed by Muima A. Shinault-Small, "A Selected Chronology of the Atlantic Beach Historical Society." The final act of that weekend was to donate to the Avery Research Center in Charleston the historical society collection of materials and photographs.

In 2009, ABHS, a sponsor, with Wachovia Bank, attended the San Diego Black Historical Society Film Festival with *VALA: The Power of Black Students at Columbia University: 1968–2008*, featuring South Carolina with many Atlantic Beach ties. It was produced by Columbia alumna and ABHS historian Sherry Suttles. The release of this book marks the 75th anniversary of the creation of Atlantic Beach.

INDEX

Atlantic Beach Christian Methodist Episcopal (CME), 8, 93, 111, 126
Atlantic Beach Company, 11, 12, 14, 15, 80, 83, 110, 113
black beaches, 33, 38–41, 64, 106, 108
black bikers, 54, 55, 117
Claflin College, South Carolina State, 11, 13, 20, 21, 66, 67, 96, 100
Cooper, 16, 17
Daniels, 34, 43–56, 59–61, 103
DeWitt, 34, 96, 97
Dixon, 16, 34, 97, 108, 117
Dozier, 12, 50, 52, 125
Fayetteville, 11, 15, 65, 67, 68, 75, 83, 102, 121
First Missionary Baptist Church, 24, 27, 30, 31, 62, 81, 83, 100, 102, 112
Fitzgerald, Charlie, 27
Floyd, 13, 22, 31, 32, 47, 51, 121
Gantt, Keenan Plan, 41, 81, 99
Gibson, 15, 30
Glass, 28–30, 53, 97
Gordon, Robert K., 11, 15–17, 33, 110
Gore/Simpson, 34, 37, 49, 57, 58, 60, 63, 73, 76, 82–92, 106, 107, 111, 113, 114
Graham, AfroFest, 23, 118, 126
Gullah/Geechee, 70–74, 120
Housing Authority, 28, 29, 75, 79, 102, 110–114, 119
Hurricane Hazel, 17, 32, 33, 104
Hurricane Hugo, 25, 32, 103
Isom, 27, 34, 50, 53, 76, 78, 82, 112, 123
Jenkins, 36, 37, 53, 82
Johnson, 20–22,29, 76, 96
Kelly, 12, 13, 15, 16
KKK, 27
Lewis, Jim, 34–36, 42, 74, 97, 102, 110
Lewis, Willie, 70–74
Marshall, 32, 33, 51, 60, 78, 108, 109
McIver, Leslie H., 66, 99
Mitchell, 34, 64, 82, 64, 102, 107
military, 68, 69
Montgomery, Mayor, 97, 99, 102
Myrtle Beach, 15, 17, 18, 19, 26, 27, 38, 40, 41, 54–56, 58, 68, 69, 89, 93, 98, 104, 105, 114–118, 121
NAACP, 10, 12, 55, 96, 102
North Myrtle Beach, 24–26, 35, 41, 44, 61, 82, 93, 100, 104, 107, 114, 116, 120, 122
Ocean Boulevard, 107
Richardson, 99, 105
Rowell, 33, 34, 51, 56, 68, 78, 79, 84, 94, 108, 109, 111, 126
Rucker, 27, 34, 53, 66, 97, 98, 102
Scott, Billy, 57, 119, 123
Seabrook, 11, 15
shag, 58, 61
Simmons, 23, 24, 28, 29, 30, 59, 97, 98, 101, 102
Sketers/Skeeters, 27, 34, 35, 57, 97, 100, 105, 122, 124, 126
Smith, W. K., 27, 28, 32, 34, 51
Stanley, 22, 23, 24, 26–31, 41, 58–60, 62, 64, 67, 68, 73, 80, 98, 101, 108, 111
Stevens, Mayor, 80, 100, 101
Vereen, *The Black Pearl*, 27, 35, 42, 56, 60, 78, 101
Tyson, George W. and Roxie Ballen, 9, 10, 125
Williams, Hubert Jr., 31, 113
Williams, Maurice, 125

BIBLIOGRAPHY

Bedford, Dr. A. Goff. *The Independent Republic: A Survey History of Horry County, South Carolina*, second edition. Myrtle Beach, SC: Horry County Historical Society, 1989.

Carter, W. Horace. *Views of Fear.* Tabor City, NC: Atlantic Publishing Company, 1991.

Floyd, Blanche W. *Tales along the King's Highway of South Carolina.* Winston-Salem, NC: Bandit Books, 1999.

Lewis, Catherine H. *Horry County, South Carolina: 1730–1993.* Columbia, SC: University of South Carolina Press, 1998.

Moredock, Will. *Banana Republic: A Year in the Heart of Myrtle Beach.* Charleston, SC: Frontline Press, Ltd., 2003.

Wells, Randall A. *Swamp, Strand & Steamboat: Voices of Horry County, South Carolina, 1732–1954.* Myrtle Beach, SC: Horry County Historical Society, 50th Anniversary Coastal Carolina University, Sheriar Press, 2004.

Wells, Randall. *Oral History Project of Horry County.* Myrtle Beach, SC: Kimbel Library, Coastal Carolina University Library, 1989–1996.

www.cofc.edu/avery/

www.hiltonheadisland.com

www.nps.gov

www.theprophets.com